WALKIN

—

WHARFEDALE

HILLSIDE GUIDES - ACROSS THE NORTH AND BEYOND

The Uplands of Britain - full colour hardback books
- THE HIGH PEAKS OF ENGLAND & WALES
- YORKSHIRE DALES, MOORS & FELLS

Hillwalking - Lake District
- LAKELAND FELLS - SOUTH
- LAKELAND FELLS - EAST
- LAKELAND FELLS - NORTH
- LAKELAND FELLS - WEST

Long Distance Walks
- COAST TO COAST WALK
- DALES WAY
- CLEVELAND WAY
- WESTMORLAND WAY
- FURNESS WAY
- LADY ANNE'S WAY
- BRONTE WAY
- CALDERDALE WAY
- PENDLE WAY
- CUMBRIA WAY
- NIDDERDALE WAY
- TRANS-PENNINE WAY

Circular Walks - Yorkshire Dales
- WHARFEDALE
- MALHAMDALE
- SWALEDALE
- NIDDERDALE
- THREE PEAKS COUNTRY
- WENSLEYDALE
- HOWGILL FELLS
- HARROGATE & WHARFE VALLEY

Circular Walks - Peak District
- NORTHERN PEAK
- CENTRAL PEAK
- EASTERN PEAK
- SOUTHERN PEAK
- WESTERN PEAK

Circular Walks - Lancashire
- BOWLAND
- PENDLE & THE RIBBLE
- WEST PENNINE MOORS

Circular Walks - North Pennines
- TEESDALE
- EDEN VALLEY
- ALSTON & ALLENDALE

Circular Walks - North York Moors
- WESTERN MOORS
- SOUTHERN MOORS

Circular Walks - South Pennines
- ILKLEY MOOR
- BRONTE COUNTRY
- CALDERDALE
- SOUTHERN PENNINES

WayMaster Visitor Guides
- YORKSHIRE DALES

---

*Send for a detailed current catalogue and price list
and also visit www.hillsidepublications.co.uk*

WALKING COUNTRY

—

WHARFEDALE

Paul Hannon

—

Hillside

HILLSIDE
PUBLICATIONS
12 Broadlands
Shann Park
Keighley
West Yorkshire
BD20 6HX

First published 1985
Fully Revised (10th) edition 2006

ISBN 1 870141 79 2

Cover illustration: Descending to Kettlewell from The Slit
Back cover: Crook Gill; Linton; Kilnsey Crag
Page One: Mock Beggar Hall, Appletreewick
Page Three: Hag Dyke, Great Whernside
(Paul Hannon/Hillslides Picture Library)

The sketch maps in this book are based upon
1947 Ordnance Survey One-Inch maps

Printed in Great Britain by
Carnmor Print
95-97 London Road
Preston
Lancashire
PR1 4BA

CONTENTS

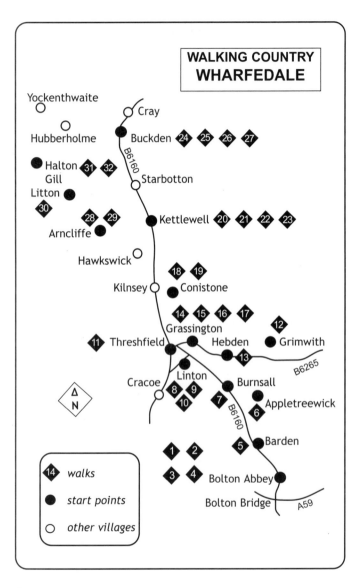

WALKING COUNTRY
WHARFEDALE

Yockenthwaite

Cray

Hubberholme

Buckden 24 25 26 27

B6160

Halton 31 32
Gill

Starbotton

Litton
30

Kettlewell 20 21 22 23

28 29

Arncliffe

Hawkswick

18 19

Kilnsey Conistone

14 15 16 17

Grassington

12

Threshfield Hebden Grimwith

11

13

B6265

Cracoe Linton Burnsall

8 9

10 7 Appletreewick

6

Barden

1 2 5

3 4 Bolton Abbey

Bolton Bridge A59

△
N

14 *walks*

● *start points*

○ *other villages*

6

INTRODUCTION

The subject of this book is the upper valley of the River Wharfe, from the boundary of the Yorkshire Dales National Park at Bolton Bridge to the heart of the Park beyond Buckden: included is the quieter side valley of Littondale. Wharfedale is an immensely beautiful valley, and is probably the most popular in the Dales, due not least of all to its accessibility. The West Yorkshire cities of Leeds and Bradford and their surrounding towns are but a modest distance away, and on summer weekends the banks of the river can see as many tourists and sun-worshippers as ramblers.

The Wharfe's name originates from the Celtic meaning 'swift water', and this lovely river races for almost 30 miles from Beckermonds to Bolton Bridge before a rather more sedate run to join the Ouse near Selby. At Beckermonds the Wharfe is formed by the confluence of Oughtershaw and Greenfield Becks, which have themselves already covered some distance from the lonely heights of Cam Fell. The Wharfe's major tributary is the Skirfare, which flows through - and sometimes beneath - its own dale, Littondale, to lose its identity near the famous landmark of Kilnsey Crag. Though Littondale has many characteristics of its big brother, it is separated by steep sided fells and its seclusion gives it an intimate, possibly even greater charm.

North of Kilnsey the valley floors are dead flat and never more than half a mile wide, and at a very clearly defined boundary the fells begin their majestic rise to numerous 2000-foot summits. At regular intervals their slopes are scored by crystal clear mountain becks which have a short lived but very joyful journey. While the higher tops display the gritstone features of peat groughs and ever moist terrain, the lower slopes show off the ever fascinating scars of gleaming limestone. The entrance to the dale is guarded by the huge gritstone portals of Barden Moor and Fell. These extensive areas of rolling heather moorland face each other across the Wharfe, overlooking the finest wooded riverside paths between Bolton Abbey and Grassington.

While the industry of the dale has always featured farming, the 19th century was the heyday of lead mining. Small operations existed all over the place, though the greatest concentration was on Grassington Moor. Their remains are evident today in spoil heaps, ruined smelt mills and kilns, shafts and levels.

Access to the countryside

The majority of the walks in this guide are on public rights of way or long-established access areas and concession paths. The implementation of 'Right to Roam' in 2004 has had little effect on the walks, several of which already made use of existing access areas and paths on Barden Moor and Fell. These now largely fall within these vast swathes of open country, and on most days of the year you are free to walk responsibly over these wonderful landscapes. These access areas were negotiated decades ago with the Duke of Devonshire's estates, a successful arrangement that must have been anathema to landowners who until 2004 had denied our heritage. Certainly the sheep and nesting birds appear unperturbed, though the grouse tend to get restless when August arrives.

Two notable restrictions are that dogs are normally banned from grouse moors other than on rights of way; and the areas can be closed to walkers for up to 28 days per year, subject to advance notice. Most likely times will be from the 'Glorious Twelfth', the start of the grouse shooting season in August, though weekends should seldom be affected. Information should be available from the Countryside Agency and either Grassington National Park Centre or the estate office (see opposite). Notices are posted at access points. Of course there are now many other areas of upland to explore, offering scope for extending or amending many walks: Open Country is clearly depicted on up-to-date OS Explorer maps.

Using the guide

Each walk is self contained, with essential information being followed by a concise route description and simple map. Dovetailed in between are notes and illustrations of features along the way. Snippets of information have been placed in *italics* to ensure that the essential route description is easier to locate. The sketch maps serve to identify the location of the routes rather than the fine detail, and whilst the description should be sufficient to guide you around, an Ordnance Survey map is strongly recommended.

To gain the most from a walk, the detail of the 1:25,000 scale Explorer map is unsurpassed. It also gives the option to vary walks, giving an improved picture of your surroundings and availability of linking paths. Just two maps cover all the walks in this book:
• *Explorer OL2 - Yorkshire Dales South/West*
• *Explorer OL30 - Yorkshire Dales North/Central*
Also useful for planning are Landranger maps 98, 99, 103 and 104.

USEFUL ADDRESSES

Ramblers' Association
2nd Floor, Camelford House, 87-89 Albert Embankment, London SE1 7BR
• 020-7339 8500

Yorkshire Dales National Park
Colvend, Hebden Road, Grassington, Skipton BD23 5LB
• 01756-752748

National Park Centre
Hebden Road **Grassington** BD23 5LB • 01756-752774

Tourist Information Centres

35 Coach Street **Skipton** BD23 1LQ • 01756-792809

Town Hall, Station Road **Ilkley** LS29 8HB • 01943-602319

Yorkshire Tourist Board
312 Tadcaster Road, York YO2 2HF
• 01904-707961

Yorkshire Dales Society
Civic Centre, Cross Green, Otley LS21 1HD
• 01943-461938

Open Access
Helpline • 0845-100 3298, *or* www.countrysideaccess.gov.uk

Bolton Abbey estate office • 01756-710227

Public Transport Information

Traveline • 0870 608 2608

National Rail Enquiries • 08457-48495

1

SIMON'S SEAT

START *Bolton Abbey*   *Grid ref. SE 077552*

DISTANCE *8$\frac{1}{2}$ miles (13$\frac{1}{2}$km)*

ORDNANCE SURVEY MAPS
1:50,000
Landranger 104 - Leeds, Bradford & Harrogate
1:25,000
Explorer OL2 - Yorkshire Dales South/West

ACCESS *Start from the Cavendish Pavilion, off the B6160 just north of Bolton Abbey, turning off by the large memorial fountain. Car park. The B6160 is served by Ilkley-Bolton Abbey-Grassington bus.• OPEN ACCESS - see page 9*

> *A super expedition through colourful country to a grand airy top*

The Cavendish Pavilion stands on the riverbank at the entrance to Strid Wood. The Pavilion has been replaced in recent years, and offers all manner of refreshments. There is also a gift shop and WC. Leave the Pavilion by crossing the wooden bridge over the Wharfe and taking a broad path upstream. Entering trees it crosses a stile and immediately forks. Take the upper one to join a back road. Turn left on this as it climbs to a brow, with an alternative parallel path. Here forsake the road for a gate set back on the right, where begins the permissive path leading to the access area. An inviting green track heads left past the isolated Waterfall Cottage to a gate, from where a now firmer track winds along to fade alongside a pond, with Posforth Gill just in front in the Valley of Desolation. *This title could not be less appropriate to the colourful terrain here, but it refers to the aftermath of a great storm in 1826.*

Turn right to run along the rim of the steep drop to the beck, noting a cameo viewpoint for a super waterfall. *In the height of summer this can be obscured by foliage, but the only alternative involves dropping to the beck a little earlier to wander upstream for a close-up view.* The usual path resumes high above the beck to quickly arrive at a tiny footbridge on it. Across, it continues more narrowly along the valley floor, soon reaching a fork. Although the main way rises left, a brief diversion is recommended on the thin path continuing upstream to enjoy an equally lovely waterfall. The main path, meanwhile, runs briefly parallel then rises to a gate into Laund Pasture Plantation. A broad track ascends rapidly to the far end of the trees, where a gate admits onto a corner of the open moor/access area.

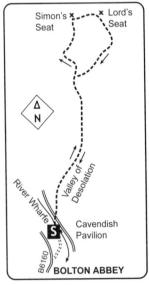

Two good tracks head away: ignore that to the left, and head directly away on the wallside track, a super green way alongside a wall. Great Agill Beck is soon crossed prior to a steep, stony section, after which the climbing is all but finished. At a stone table Truckle Crags and more distantly Simon's Seat come into view. Beyond the table a shooters' track branches off to the right: this is where you rejoin the outward route on returning from the top. For now, follow the broad ascending path which crosses the headwaters of the beck at Great Agill Head before swinging right at a fork to pass Truckle Crags, and the large grouping of rocks atop Simon's Seat are only minutes away on a peaty but generally dry path. The environs of the summit are a source of potential confusion in bad visibility, but the main path makes directly for the highest point. *At 1591ft/485m the unmistakable form of an Ordnance Survey column adorns the highest rocks, and to add interest to the final few feet, hands must be used to attain it. The giant boulders of Simon's Seat*

make an ideal playground for scramblers, though the great walls of rock falling to the north from below the summit are strictly the preserve of rock climbers.

The view from Simon's Seat is made unforgettable by virtue of the fact that your sheltered line of approach has kept all to the north hidden until the last moment. Along with the anticipated panorama of much of the Dales is a dramatic bird's-eye view of the valley, a result of the unbroken plunge of the northern slope of the fell. The environs of Skyreholme and Appletreewick form a fine picture, with Trollers Gill, Parcevall Hall and Grimwith Reservoir all easily located. A nice section of the Wharfe can also be seen.

To vary the return take the initially sketchy path heading east to the prominent boss of rock at Lord's Seat. Almost at once this transforms into a stone flagged trod, which ends abruptly halfway along, leaving you on a moist, peaty little path. This runs to the Lord's Seat outcrops which offer much scrambling fun, and to a wall just beyond. Turn right on a path alongside the wall to commence a gradual descent. After the confinement of the ascent route, wide open spaces now abound. After a while a neat track takes over, soon reaching a junction. Here turn sharp right as the wide track undulates across the moor past various scattered rocks, and leads unfailingly back to the outward route near the stone table. Steps can now be happily retraced all the way back to the Pavilion.

Ascending Simon's Seat Opposite: waterfall, Valley of Desolation

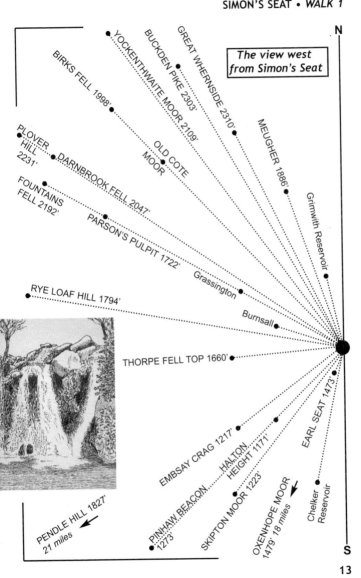

The view west from Simon's Seat

N

YOCKENTHWAITE MOOR 2109'

BUCKDEN PIKE 2303'

GREAT WHERNSIDE 2310'

BIRKS FELL 1998'

MEUGHER 1886'

OLD COTE MOOR

PLOVER HILL 2231'

DARNBROOK FELL 2047'

Grimwith Reservoir

FOUNTAINS FELL 2192'

PARSON'S PULPIT 1722'

Grassington

RYE LOAF HILL 1794'

Burnsall

THORPE FELL TOP 1660'

EARL SEAT 1473'

EMBSAY CRAG 1217'

HALTON HEIGHT 1171'

Chelker Reservoir

PENDLE HILL 1827' 21 miles

PINHAW BEACON 1273'

SKIPTON MOOR 1223

OXENHOPE MOOR 1479' 18 miles

S

13

2

BOLTON ABBEY

START Bolton Abbey   Grid ref. SE 077552

DISTANCE 4^{1}2 miles (7km)

ORDNANCE SURVEY MAPS
1:50,000
Landranger 104 - Leeds, Bradford & Harrogate
1:25,000
Explorer OL2 - Yorkshire Dales South/West

ACCESS Start from the Cavendish Pavilion, off the B6160 just north of Bolton Abbey, turning off by the large memorial fountain. Large car park. The B6160 is served by Ilkley-Bolton Abbey-Grassington bus.

A simple riverside stroll on good paths in fine surroundings. The central feature, in sight for most of the walk, is the hoary old ruin of Upper Wharfedale's most famous building.

The Cavendish Pavilion stands at the riverbank entrance to Strid Wood. It offers all manner of refreshments, with a gift shop and WC alongside. From the Pavilion set off back along the drive, but go left into the car park and follow a track along the Wharfe's bank. When the track ends a path goes on through a gate, then with the priory just across the river, the path swings right to climb to a gate to emerge onto the road at the Cavendish memorial fountain. *This commemorates Lord Frederick Cavendish, assassinated in Phoenix Park, Dublin in 1882 (Cavendish is the family name of the Dukes of Devonshire, long-time owners of the estate).* Turn left to quickly reach a gate into the priory grounds. The most direct route back towards the river is through the graveyard, but few will not halt to explore the ruins and the priory church.

Bolton Abbey is, strictly, the name for the tiny village whose showpiece is more correctly the Priory. The imposing ruin forms a magnet for close-at-hand West Yorkshire visitors, with the river hereabouts being an attraction in its own right. The priory dates from 1154 and was built by Augustinian canons who moved here from nearby Embsay. At the Dissolution the nave was spared, and remains to this day the parish church. Much else of interest in the vicinity includes adjacent Bolton Hall, dating from the 17th century. Up on the main road are Post office, shop, tearooms, bookshop, WC and a large and splendid example of a tithe barn.

On arriving at the wooden bridge and its adjacent stepping-stones do not be tempted to cross, but instead follow the riverbank downstream again. A long, pleasant pasture leads all the way to Bolton Bridge. As the old bridge appears ahead, the sprawling Devonshire Arms Hotel appears to the right, and through a kissing-gate there is an option to cross directly to it. A tearoom stands across the road. A delightfully sited cricket pitch is passed to join the old road alongside the bridge. *The shapely bridge marks the Wharfe's departure from the National Park, and completion of the 1994 by-pass at last left this splendid old crossing in peace. The extension of a steam railway from Embsay has seen Bolton Abbey's restored station back in use, situated a long half-mile along the A59 towards Skipton.*

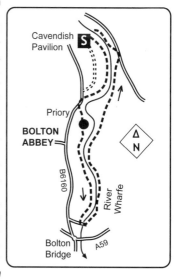

Cross the bridge, and just beyond a cottage turn left along an enclosed pathway before Red Lion Farm, to enter a riverside pasture. As the Wharfe is neared the grassy way is deflected above a steep, wooded bank, and from a stile at the end it drops back down to cross long flat pastures parallel with the river. After a tiny stream and a stile another wooded bank intervenes. A steep field is climbed, remaining with the left-hand fence to a stile at the end, then on just a little further to a superb high-level vantage point which reveals the priory ruins in style.

Just past a stile is a path junction. The main one slants down the bank to a T-junction, where the right branch is followed. Alternatively, simply remain on the bank top as a nicer, thin path runs on the wallside to meet the ascending main path. Now simply follow this on a splendid high-level course along the top of the wooded bank, at the end emerging onto a narrow road as it drops to ford Pickles Beck: a footbridge caters for dry-shod pedestrians. On the other side a stile gives access to a riverbank path for the final few minutes back to the Pavilion bridge.

Bolton Priory from across the Wharfe

STRID WOOD

START Bolton Abbey   Grid ref. SE 077552

DISTANCE 5 miles (8km)

ORDNANCE SURVEY MAPS
1:50,000
Landranger 104 - Leeds, Bradford & Harrogate
1:25,000
Explorer OL2 - Yorkshire Dales South/West

ACCESS Start from the Cavendish Pavilion, off the B6160 just north of Bolton Abbey, turning off by the large memorial fountain. Large car park. The B6160 is served by Ilkley-Bolton Abbey-Grassington bus.

> An outstanding juxtaposition of river and woodland, and an absolute riot of autumn colour

This delectable section of the Wharfe is part of the Duke of Devonshire's Bolton Abbey estate, and a combination of largely permissive paths allows good access to both banks. With the exception of the Pavilion to Posforth Bridge all paths are private, though 'the public are invited to walk and picnic' in a manner that captures the Victorian flavour still evident hereabouts. The Pavilion itself has been replaced in recent years, and offers all manner of refreshments. There is also a gift shop and WC.

Other than at the Strid it is the woodland itself that steals the show from the river. Strid Wood is a very popular riverside habitat where man and nature appear to happily co-exist. The importance of the woodland for birds and plants is recognised by designation as a Site of Special Scientific Interest (SSSI) and this should be respected by keeping to paths. This should not pose any problems, *for a splendid network laid out in the 19th century, has been well maintained ever since. Today the paths have been upgraded to the point where you could almost walk the route in your Sunday shoes.*

From the Pavilion cross the wooden bridge and turn upstream. At a stile into woodland the path forks: remain on the riverbank, crossing a footbridge adjacent to the road bridge on Posforth Gill. The path clings to the river until faced with a surprisingly sustained pull to the top of the wood. Here awaits a well-sited rest house. *Bedecked with a luxuriant bilberry thatch, this up-market seat occupies the first of several well-chosen viewpoints.* Hereafter, easy walking ensues on a magnificent terrace. One particular glimpse gives a surprise cameo of the Strid, perfectly framed by foliage.

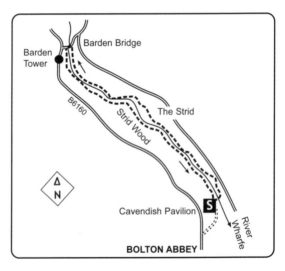

Shortly afterwards comes another classic moment, as the High Strid is revealed in a contrastingly open setting. The path leaves the wood at a stile to descend to the riverbank at an aqueduct. *This impressive structure was built to carry a water pipeline from the Nidderdale reservoirs to the taps of Bradford: it also carries a path, thus if the heavens open you might use it as a short-cut back into the shelter of Strid Wood.* The continuing path runs on the riverbank to arrive at Barden Bridge, which is revealed well in advance. Before crossing, note the old tablet set into it. *Barden lays claim to the Wharfe's finest bridge, and the tablet dates its restoration 'at the charge of the whole West Riding' as 1676. Those with time to spare will enjoy a detour up the road after crossing the bridge, for just two minutes above, and accessed by a stile in the wall part way up, are the ruins of Barden Tower (see page 24).*

Back at the bridge a stile kicks off the return leg, emerging from trees for an open spell past the aqueduct. On entering Strid Wood remain on the main path, keeping left at any junctions to see the High Strid on the river and a rock pinnacle (the Hawkstone) above the rocky path. Either way the Strid itself, further downstream, cannot be missed. The Strid is the focal point of the wood, as the Wharfe is forced through a narrow gritstone channel of great depth. *Lives have been lost here in senseless attempts to leap the foaming waters. Many decades ago visitors could travel here in style, by wagonette from the old railway station. A path climbing to the right leads up to the Strid car park, with refreshments, shop and WC.* The broad carriageway created for early visitors now leads gently back all the way to the Cavendish Pavilion, a couple of late branches offering closer spells with the river.

Barden Tower

4

HAZLEWOOD MOOR

START Bolton Abbey   Grid ref. SE 077552

DISTANCE 6 miles (9½km)

ORDNANCE SURVEY MAPS
1:50,000
Landranger 104 - Leeds, Bradford & Harrogate
1:25,000
Explorer OL2 - Yorkshire Dales South/West

ACCESS Start from the village car park. Served by Grassington-Ilkley bus. • OPEN ACCESS - see page 9.

> A high level circuit of Pickles Gill on moorland tracks.
> Hazlewood Moor is only a part of this vast upland known as
> Barden Fell stretching east to Thruscross and - Simon's Seat aside
> - attracts fewer walkers than Barden Moor across the Wharfe.

For a note on Bolton Abbey village and priory, see page 15. From the car park return to the road and cross to the famous 'Hole in the Wall', through which descend with the crowds to the ever-lovely environs of the priory ruins. As a look round might be better enjoyed at the end of the walk, for now cross the wooden foot-bridge and turn upstream. Almost at once the main path bears right to gently scale the hillside. At the first opportunity take the branch doubling back up to the right to the top of the wood. *Pause to look back over a super prospect of the priory*. Through a gate in front a narrow, deeply inurned snicket whisks you away from the Bolton Abbey scene, climbing to join a track up to Bank Farm and then out along its access road to meet the minor road through tiny Storiths. *Just along to the left, at Back o'th' Hill Farm a coffee shop has refreshments and a model railway.*

20

Across the road is the pocket moor of Storiths Crag, an outlier of the access area. Directly opposite, a short-lived track heads off past a cottage. It quickly narrows to a path to rise up a wallside to meet a stony drive. Turn left along this to approach Town End Farm, then bear right over a cattle-grid onto the open moor. *Already you have grand views, with a section of the river down by the Cavendish Pavilion, and Barden Moor behind.* A little further, keep straight on (the right branch) at a fork for the track to begin a steady pull towards the heights through bilberry surrounds.

As height is gained the intake wall returns, and at another fork (Intake farm drive) your route takes the initially less appealing way to the right. This green track soon perks up to head straight on as a similar track comes in from the right, now entirely amid heather. Down to the left are a handful of fields encircling Intake Farm. *The rocky crown of Simon's Seat looms to the north.* Keep on through a gate in a fence, after which a track climbs from the farm to briefly join

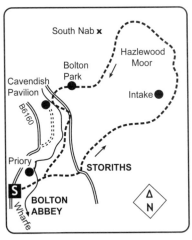

your track: take no notice as it resumes its climb to the right. Your route now begins a steady drop towards Pickles Gill Beck, reaching the stream at an old stone sheepfold in a setting that begs a halt.

Across the ford the path makes a short, steep climb before easing out to undulate along to a junction. *At 1115ft/340m, this is the highest point of the walk and a grand one too. The view includes Beamsley Beacon, Rombalds Moor, the South Pennines, Boulsworth Hill, Pendle Hill, Longridge Fell and the Bowland moors. Also in view is the priory itself, in its delectable green set- ting on the valley floor. Just to your right is a bilberry-roofed luncheon hut amid a scattering of boulders: definitely a place for a refreshment halt, it's all downhill from here.* Go down to the left to quickly reach Hammerthorn Gate, meeting a harder track coming in from the right to leave the moor together. *On the knoll to the right an Ordnance Survey column set back from South Nab may tempt a detour.* Continue down the stony track, through a reedy pasture then fields to the attractive farmhouse of Bolton Park. Passing right of the buildings, its drive leads down to a back road.

Cross straight over to the wooden bridge on the Wharfe. *Arrival at the Cavendish Pavilion is a severe culture shock after the open moor, with cafe, shop, WC, and big crowds, more often than not!* If not succumbing to the temptations, then take the nearside riverbank path downstream. At the far end of the pasture you are deflected onto the road to negotiate Pickles Beck, with a footbridge upstream of the ford. On the other side a very brief pull sees a firm path turn into the trees on the right. This winds a splendid course along the top of the steep, wooded bank, before long reaching a fork just beyond a wooden viewpoint seat. Prior to this you pass a fallen tree entirely embedded with hammered coins.

Either choice will lead unfailingly to the priory footbridge, though the higher one offers a more rewarding trek with some splendid views through the trees. A second money tree is passed, while springtime brings a good display of bluebells. The lower path slants down to the riverbank, and both emerge from the woods to lovely scenes of the priory just ahead, most memorably from the upper path. This now slants down to the bottom, to conclude at the footbridge. As the lower one emerges you can opt to trace the loop of the riverbank back to the bridge to cross and explore the priory.

The Hole in the Wall, Bolton Abbey

BARDEN MOOR

START Barden   Grid ref. SE 052573

DISTANCE 8 miles (13km)

ORDNANCE SURVEY MAPS
1:50,000
Landranger 104 - Leeds, Bradford & Harrogate
1:25,000
Explorer OL2 - Yorkshire Dales South/West

ACCESS Start from Barden Bridge. Riverside parking area, and the adjacent field is often opened up. Barden is served by Ilkley-Bolton Abbey-Grassington bus. • OPEN ACCESS - see page 9.

> *Easy walking through a rich moorland tapestry,*
> *topped off with a riverbank saunter*

NOTE BEFORE STARTING: The walk crosses the Wharfe by stepping-stones at Drebley, a potential impasse if the river is high or one's confidence is low. They are however, in good condition.

Barden Moor is a vast playground both for the rambler and the less unobtrusive 'sportsman'. Above the intake walls encircling it, bracken flanks give way to heather and rough grass, where one can follow paths and tracks or roam free. The millstone grit outcrops and edges that characterise the northern and western scarps of the moor are absent from this walk, which instead explores the heart of the moor. At Barden is the Wharfe's finest bridge. A tablet dates its restoration - 'at the charge of the whole West Riding' - as 1676. Start by crossing the bridge and up the road climbing steeply to Barden Tower. A stile gives access to the ruin, beyond which its main entrance leads out onto the B6160.

WALK 5 • BARDEN MOOR

Barden Tower was built as a hunting lodge by the powerful Cliffords of Skipton Castle, and boasted two famous Cliffords as residents. Henry the 'Shepherd' Lord came in 1485, being raised in the Cumbrian fells until the Wars of the Roses ended. Up to his death in 1523 he preferred Barden's peace and the company of the canons of Bolton to Skipton's splendour. He also had the adjacent chapel built. The redoubtable Lady Anne had the Tower restored in 1659 and spent much of her final years here. In 1676 she died, last of the Cliffords, and the long process of decay set in. The chapel now serves as a restaurant.

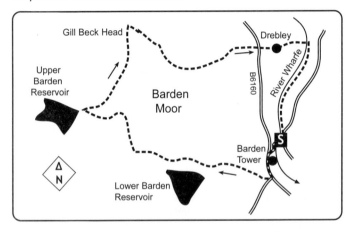

On leaving, turn left along the road to the Embsay turning. Only yards up it, escape by a gate on the right to enter the access area. A hard access road heads off across the moor, rising steadily through increasing heather towards Lower Barden Reservoir. Ignore a branch left towards the dam, and continue straight up to run well above the shoreline. Beyond its head, the track starts a longer climb to the dam of its higher neighbour. *On the final pull, the lofty obelisk on Cracoe Fell (WALK 9) is seen on the skyline ahead.* Alongside the dam stands the old reservoir keepers' house.

Return a few yards to a junction where a footpath sign to Burnsall invites a foot-friendlier ramble on a more traditional moorland track. It maintains a near level course for some time, contouring splendidly round to an attractive little dam at Gill Beck Head. *This is the jewelled tarn of Barden Moor's 'Lake District', and a favourite haunt of gulls. In view from it, just up the slope, is a chimney from a former colliery, worked to supply coal for the lead smelting mill on Grassington Moor. A shooters' house stands on the skyline directly above the old chimney.*

Across the modest embankment a crossroads is reached: at 1214ft/370m this is the highest point of the walk. Turn right on a track through the heather, running along to meet a similar track by some grouse butts. Once again keep right, this one drops down to a distinct fork. Now bear left, soon becoming delightful underfoot as the track runs along towards the moor edge. Beyond a gate in a fence the heather finally gives way to small boulders on a grassy knoll. *This is a good place to take stock, with a marvellous prospect over the little huddle of Drebley, across the valley to Howgill and the deep bowl of the Appletreewick-Skyreholme area all in the shadow of Simon's Seat.* Below, the track slants down to the head of a green lane, at which point the access area is left. The walled lane descends directly to the B6160 Burnsall road.

Almost opposite, the access road to Drebley offers immediate escape as it resumes your drop towards the river. *Drebley itself is a timeless farming community that was once a forest lodge.* After the first building (an elegant house of 1830) turn into the tidy farmyard on the left, continuing straight through a couple of gates at the end to emerge on a level track. As it quickly forks, take the right branch through a gate ahead. Part way along the field top turn right, down through a gate in the wall below and down again to gain the Wharfe's bank precisely at the stepping-stones.

Drebley's stepping-stones display much character: a refusal will incur three penalty points and more importantly retraced steps, for there is no path in either direction on Drebley's bank of the Wharfe. Those of a nervous disposition will find no solace in the knowledge that a footbridge existed here decades ago. On the east bank is a barn that was formerly Hough Mill, restored by Lady Anne Clifford, in 1657. Moving swiftly to the opposite bank (on paper, at least) the final stage of the walk is very straightforward, tracing a beautiful and tranquil reach of the Wharfe downstream to Barden Bridge. Barden Tower quickly appears in the trees ahead, an indication of the walk's near conclusion.

TROLLERS GILL

START *Appletreewick*   *Grid ref. SE 053601*

DISTANCE *7½ miles (12km)*

ORDNANCE SURVEY MAPS
1:50,000
Landranger 98 - Wensleydale & Upper Wharfedale
Landranger 99 - Northallerton & Ripon
Landranger 104 - Leeds, Bradford & Harrogate
1:25,000
Explorer OL2 - Yorkshire Dales South/West

ACCESS *Start from the village centre. Limited roadside parking: during the season a large meadow near the village centre provides car parking. Served by Ilkley-Bolton Abbey-Grassington bus.*

> *Exceptional river scenery precedes one of Craven's best limestone features*

For a note on Appletreewick see page 32. Leave by heading west out of the village on the Burnsall road, past the two pubs and Low Hall to reach a walled path leading past a campsite to the Wharfe. Turn left alongside the river, meeting an early interruption as a steep, wooded bank deflects the path up wooden steps before returning to the riverbank. Now the Wharfe is faithfully traced through a couple of pastures before entering a delightfully wooded section. At its far end note the simple but touching memorial plate set into a rock. Emerging into a field, the path forsakes the river by bearing left to a track out onto a narrow road at a bridge.

Cross the bridge and leave the road in favour of an enclosed track up to the left. Beyond a gorgeous cottage it narrows to meet Howgill Lane at the top, alongside the farm at Howgill. Turn left along the unsurfaced lane past the caravan site at Howgill Lodge, whose little shop offers refreshments. A little beyond a converted barn look out for an old milestone set into the wall. *It points the way to 'Patley Bridge 6', indicating the lane's former importance.* At this point leave by a gate opposite and follow an old green way along the wallside, first on its right, then its left. After a gateway, with Skyreholme straight ahead, slope down to a stile in the next wall, and continue down to cross a tiny beck at an old wall. With Skyreholme Beck just to the left advance along the field to arrive at a footbridge on it. *Just before this a well preserved limekiln stands across to the right.* Over the bridge suburban steps ascend to a housing development to emerge onto the road at Skyreholme.

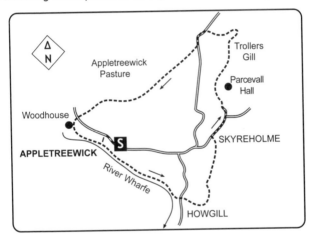

Turn right along this quiet road past the delectable frontage of Lane House Farm, quickly dropping to a junction at a bridge, phone box and seat. Fork left here to the road end at the entrance to Parcevall Hall. *This is the grandest house in Upper Wharfedale. Built over 300 years ago, its beautiful stonework looks out across Skyreholme to Simon's Seat, which totally dominates this corner of the valley. Now used as a diocesan retreat centre, the gardens and intermingled woodland are open to the public from Easter to October (fee payable), and there is also a tearoom.*

Take the gate before the wooden bridge to follow Skyreholme Beck upstream on a good path through several more gates. A stile beyond a barn admits to Open Country, and this colourful enclosure features the grassy retaining wall of a reservoir. *Made to serve the mills of Skyreholme, both dam and mills are now history.* Beyond another stile the path forks in the amphitheatre just short of Trollers Gill. The high wedge of Middle Hill divides the gorge from its parallel valley to the left: it is through this deep side valley that the right of way continues, but the choice to make is right, on the main path which curves into the open, stony surrounds which only at the last moment reveal the secretive entrance to the limestone gorge that is Trollers Gill. *Though not particularly tall, the cliffs remain unbroken for some distance, and the narrow passage between is usually dry. It is renowned as home of the legendary 'Barguest', a spectral hound with eyes like saucers!*

Emerging at the other end, simply continue along the shallow trough, the tiny stream probably re-appearing before you reach a ladder-stile further on. Just past it, cross the stream to a ladder-stile over which a permissive path ascends the little bank and runs pleasantly on to drop to meet a grassy former miners' track. Turn right on this, very briefly, and before reaching a sharp bend, leave on a grassy path ascending the slope ahead. Just down to the right is the deep pothole of Hell Hole. The grand path runs on above a circular pool to reach a wall-stile onto the back road from Appletreewick up to the Pateley Bridge road.

Follow this road left, and a little beyond a bend take a gate on the right: this is further along the road than the map suggests. A wide, stony track crosses the broad upland of Appletreewick Pasture. *This high point of the walk boasts an extensive panorama including, clockwise, Barden Moor, the Malhamdale hills, Old Cote Moor, Grassington Moor, Great Whernside and Simon's Seat. Further along, a more intimate picture of the river's environs is revealed.* Eventually the track drops gently down to enter a short-lived walled section. Unless time is pressing ignore the Appletreewick sign at the path crossroads at the end, and take the gate directly ahead to run alongside a wall to a cluster of modern barns. To their right an initially enclosed, delectable green track heads away, soon opening out to commence its descent. *Just ahead, Hartlington Hall stands embowered in trees, while further down you pass an old circular dewpond created to slake the thirst of cattle in these limestone surrounds.* The track winds down to join the Appletreewick-Burnsall road.

Cross straight over and down the access track to Woodhouse Farm. *This 17th century manor house has an attractive mullioned windowed frontage in an enviable setting.* Turn left between the buildings to make a bee-line for the riverbank. All that remains is to accompany the Wharfe downstream, partly through woodland, to return to the enclosed path by which you gained the river at the start of the walk. Retrace those early steps to finish.

Trollers Gill

7

DIBBLE'S BRIDGE

START Burnsall   Grid ref. SE 032611

DISTANCE 6 miles (9½km)

ORDNANCE SURVEY MAPS
1:50,000
Landranger 98 - Wensleydale & Upper Wharfedale
1:25,000
Explorer OL2 - Yorkshire Dales South/West

ACCESS Start from the village centre. Car park at the entrance to the village, while a riverside meadow is also often opened up. Served by Ilkley-Grassington bus.

> *A circuit of Barben Beck over gently rolling hills, with a fine stretch of the Wharfe to finish*

For a note on Burnsall see page 34. Leave by crossing the bridge and using steep steps on the left to descend to the Wharfe. After two stiles near the river, climb directly up the very steep field to a stile onto narrow Skuff Road. *A splendid retrospective view is earned of Burnsall backed by its fell.* From the stile opposite, climb another field to a stile and then on to a choice of stiles: ignore one in front, and take the one in the very corner. Now rise diagonally across a large field to a stile onto another road. Turn up it past Raikes Farm only as far as a sharp bend, and leave by a stile directly ahead. After a rise up two fieldsides, the brow of Langerton Hill is gained just below its highest point.

Resume along the wallside, soon crossing it at a stile. *Ahead is the big grassy dam of Grimwith Reservoir, while across outflowing Barben Beck is your return route overtopped by Simon's Seat.* Remain near the wall to descend a large field to a tiny stream at the far end. From the stiles here rise half-right to a stile beyond a barn, then accompany a wall up to another barn. From two neighbouring stiles continue with the wall now on the left to a stile into Turf Gate Farm. Head straight on past the buildings to follow its access road out onto the B6265 Grassington-Pateley Bridge road. Turn right along here to drop down to Dibble's Bridge. *This was the scene of a tragic coach crash in 1975, when Britain's worst motoring disaster resulted in 32 fatalities. A mile north of Dibble's Bridge is the enlarged Grimwith Reservoir, which supplies Bradford. Between the reservoir and the bridge the watercourse is not Barben Beck, but the River Dibb. Covering only one mile under this guise, is it the shortest river in the country? Immediately below the bridge is a lovely solitary house, a former mill.*

After crossing the bridge a stile gives access to a beckside area of limestone outcrops, a long abandoned quarry. Vacate it by a stile in the far top corner, and slant up to a gate ahead. Continue straight across to a stile at the far end to enter the expanse of A p p l e t r e e w i c k Pasture sloping down to Barben Beck. Dropping to cross a tiny beck, note the large boulder alongside. *It contains several cup marks, Bronze Age relics of uncertain purpose.* The thin path slants up a little before commencing a long, level section on an intermittent route high above the attractive beck.

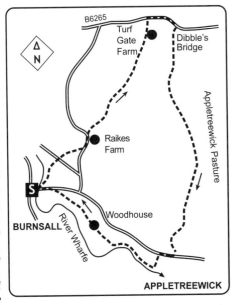

When a wall appears in front, deflect left of it to find converging walls at the top end. Escape along a short, narrow passage on the left. *During this brief section you bridge an old stone arch, the site of a tunnel used during 18th century lead mining operations.* On emerging turn right and remain with the wall, through a gate then a stile before ultimately joining an enclosed track at a path crossroads. Cross straight over to enter another narrow pasture, which is crossed by a good track to the opposite corner. It now becomes enclosed by walls to drop down onto the road at one end of Appletreewick, alongside the old village stocks, and more conveniently still, adjacent to one of the village's two pubs.

Appletreewick has several claims to fame, even though many visitors may best remember its delightful name. Here are three halls and two pubs in amongst a wonderful assortment of cottages. All stand on the narrow road wandering through the village, from High Hall at the top - note the tiny church nearby - to Low Hall at the very bottom. Probably the oldest however is the curiously named Mock Beggar Hall, a fine little edifice that once went by the title of Monk's Hall. The Craven Arms takes its name from the family of William Craven, a Dick Whittington character who found his fortune in London, becoming Lord Mayor in 1611. Not forgetting his beginnings he became a worthy local benefactor, having Burnsall's grammar school and a number of bridges in the district built. The New Inn, meanwhile, achieved national fame thanks to the enterprising 'no-smoking' policy of a 1970s landlord, long before such ideas became commonplace.

From the Craven Arms turn right (away from the village) past Low Hall to locate an enclosed path leading past a campsite to the river. Turn right to follow the Wharfe upstream. On emerging from trees the river takes a big swing to the left, and here the path is deflected right by an intervening wall to enter the farmyard at Woodhouse. *This 17th century manor house boasts an attractive frontage in an enviable setting.* When its access road turns right to join the road, go straight ahead to a footbridge. Here Barben Beck is encountered again just prior to its entry into the Wharfe. Cross a field to a stile, from where the firm path runs above a bank falling to the river, with Burnsall just ahead. As the bank fades the river undertakes another great loop, but the path simply crosses the last field to a stile at the bridge-end to finish as you began.

BURNSALL

START *Linton Falls*   *Grid ref. SE 001631*

DISTANCE *6¹4 miles (10km)*

ORDNANCE SURVEY MAPS
1:50,000
Landranger 98 - Wensleydale & Upper Wharfedale
1:25,000
Explorer OL2 - Yorkshire Dales South/West

ACCESS *Start from the National Park car park on the cul-de-sac road to Linton church. Road-end served by Ilkley-Grassington bus.*

> *An undemanding walk clinging tightly to the river*
> *after an outward leg offering fine Wharfedale views*

From the car park head along the cul-de-sac lane towards the church, but if saving its charm for the end of the walk, turn up a short enclosed way before a house on the right. At the top (ignore another way branching off) a pasture is entered, and crossed to a stile left of the barn ahead. From it rise diagonally up above the steeper drop to arrive at a stile in the distant facing wall. Two small fields then precede emergence onto the Burnsall road.

Turn right a few yards to a gate opposite and rise left to a gate in a fence at the top corner. *Very evident in the fields hereabouts, and across the river, are strip lynchets, cultivation terraces of early farmers.* Ascend slightly left again to a small gate, behind which a green snicket wends its way up to join the similarly narrow Thorpe Lane. *In an uncharacteristic lapse the Ordnance Survey has omitted to portray the snicket as the enclosed way it has clearly been for a long, long time.* Go left into Thorpe, turning right at the end to enter the hamlet. *For a note on Thorpe see page 36.*

From the centre bear left on the road out, and a little further take a rough lane on the right. At its early demise descend a slim field to a fence and down again to a stile by a trickling stream. The way rises away in a virtual straight line across three fields to reach Badger Lane, a walled track. A stile opposite resumes the fields' crossing, and after dropping down the first field a direct course for Burnsall is set. The church tower is a useful guide, while behind it, Simon's Seat dominates the skyline. More guidance is provided by a tightly bunched series of stiles, designed to test agility in addition to delaying arrival in Burnsall. The village is entered by way of a back yard, then turning right along the street into the centre.

Burnsall's setting is near perfection, with bridge, green (and maypole), church, inn and cottages fusing together into an unforgettable Wharfedale scene. St Wilfred's church dates largely from the 15th century, with a Norman font. Alongside is the village school, founded in 1602 as one of 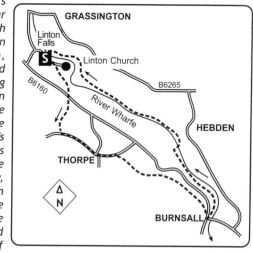 the earliest grammar schools. Along with the Red Lion Inn, tea-room, shop, WC, the Devonshire Fell Hotel overlooks the village.

Join the Wharfe by turning down between the Red Lion and the bridge, and follow a firm path upstream. It soon sees the back of the village, passing below the church and along to a knoll above the gorge of Loup Scar. Here the Wharfe rushes through an impressive limestone fault, a hugely popular short stroll. From these spectacular environs the path drops back down to the river to run through lovely wooded surroundings to the suspension bridge below

Hebden. *Just before it, note the old stone stairway known as the Postman's Steps. The suspension bridge celebrated its centenary in 1985, having been constructed to replace the stepping-stones of Hebden Hippings which themselves have since been restored.*

On the opposite bank this uncomplicated leg of the walk resumes, through a deep-set reach of the Wharfe. On emerging, a loop in the river is cut out by crossing a large pasture to the right of the tree-masked sewage works. At its access road a direct option crosses the stepping-stones ahead to reach the church. If balked, turn right along the track away from the river and up past a fish farm. As it climbs through a bend, take a stile on the left to regain the Wharfe's bank opposite Linton church. A couple of fields further and the footbridge at Linton Falls is reached and crossed.

Here the Wharfe erupts into a rare moment of anger as it tumbles over limestone boulders and ledges, a foaming sight in spate. In contrast, immediately upstream the river flows wide and calm between two weirs. To conclude, a ginnel leads back onto the road with the car park just to the left. To visit the church, keep on past it to the road end. *Enclosed in a loop of the river is the squat church of St Michael & all Angels, positioned to be central to the villages it was built to serve. Dating from Norman times, it retains 15th century work and its interior lives up to its idyllic setting.*

The Wharfe at Burnsall

THORPE FELL TOP

START *Linton*   *Grid ref. SD 997627*

DISTANCE *9 miles (14$\frac{1}{2}$km)*

ORDNANCE SURVEY MAPS
1:50,000
Landranger 98 - Wensleydale & Upper Wharfedale
Landranger 103 - Blackburn & Burnley
Landranger 104 - Leeds, Bradford & Harrogate
1:25,000
Explorer OL2 - Yorkshire Dales South/West

ACCESS *Start from the village centre. Roadside parking. Served by Skipton-Grassington bus.* • *OPEN ACCESS - see page 9*

> *A fine stretch of moorland rambling, contrasting well with the tiny villages under the steep slopes*

For a note on Linton see page 41. From the Fountaine Inn cross the green and the beck and follow the lane along to the right to its imminent demise at a farm. Don't enter but take a bridle-gate on the left, and follow the fieldside path past the house, on through a further gate, then a little further to one in the wall on the right. Joining a firm track, it climbs with the left-hand wall (past two early stiles) to a gate at the top corner. Continue on with the wall to another gate, where the track peters out. Ascending a large field, pass left of a line of trees to the remains of a barn. A stile to its left admits onto Thorpe Lane. Turn left to follow its narrow course into Thorpe, turning right at the end to drop into the hamlet.

The farming hamlet of Thorpe has an elusiveness which allegedly kept it hidden from the marauding Scots. Romantically titled 'Thorpe in the Hollow' it shelters between reef knolls and below the overpowering Thorpe Fell. Prominent in the Linton and Thorpe scene, the rounded hills known as reef knolls are of limestone with a grass covering, relics of underwater mounds exposed by the eventual erosion of overlying rocks.

Bear right at the triangular, walled green in the centre and keep on until the road dissolves into a couple of rough tracks. Opt for the left one which begins to climb steeply between walls to emerge at an access point onto the open moor. Of several sunken tracks that head directly away, the right-most one is to be preferred. This swings up to the

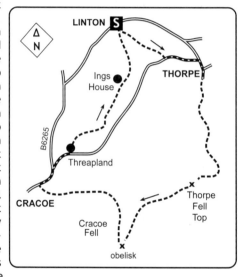

right to terminate at the remains of a small quarry. From a small cairn go left past the quarry to meet a more substantial path. On rounding the beginnings of a beck keep to the left-most, better track which regains its groove, quickly reaching a fork at a small cairn and a few rocks. Keep right to now rise more normally up a gentle slope, the way soon reforming into one final sunken section. As the groove disappears for good a stone shooting house appears ahead, and is soon reached on a good path.

At the shooting house a wider track is met. *A lesser stone hut below it offers refuge from the elements.* Rise to the big house, and just yards along the track to the right, a less firm but clear track branches left. This rises slightly and up towards shooting butts. Before reaching them, bear off right and ascend directly up the modest slope, and you will quickly espy the Ordnance Survey column on Thorpe Fell Top. At 1660ft/506m, Thorpe Fell Top is the infrequently visited summit of Barden Moor. *This huge mass is contained in a triangle bounded by the Skipton-Threshfield-Bolton Abbey roads, and consists largely of a magnificent tract of heather moorland. This gritstone landscape contrasts markedly with the limestone country at the start of the walk. Though outcropping on the summit, the boulders are most profuse where they line the rim of the plateau in typical gritstone edge fashion.*

The view is a splendid all round panorama, though devoid of any immediate interest. Some of the principal features are listed, clockwise from the east: Simon's Seat, Earl Seat, Beamsley Beacon, Rombald's Moor, Chelker Reservoir, Skipton Moor, Oxenhope Moor, Boulsworth Hill, Pendle Hill, Waddington Fell, Parlick and the Bowland moors, Malhamdale hills, Ingleborough, Fountains Fell, Birks Fell, Kilnsey Crag, Yockenthwaite Moor, Buckden Pike, Great Whernside, Grimwith Reservoir, Greenhow Hill.

Next objective is the conspicuous obelisk on Cracoe Fell, a mile distant. A thin path heads directly towards it, dropping gently down to a slightly peatier area to reach an inscribed boundary stone just short of the depression between the felltop and the monument. *It divides Cracoe and Thorpe parishes, and its 'B' side is inscribed 'DD', yet more evidence of ownership.* Just a little further another path is met alongside wooden shooting butts. Swing right in front of these to join the substantial wall along the crest of the escarpment. Now turn left on a path by the wall for an easy walk up to the monument, a stile provides access to it. *Large rocks on the near side of the wall are sufficient for playful scrambling. Cracoe's memorial to its war dead is a real Wharfedale landmark. The solid structure is made of the same rock on which it is perched, and commands a glorious view. Its moor-edge location ensures that distant Dales mountains are complemented by a rich collection of villages such as Hetton, Threshfield and Grassington. Less pleasingly, Wharfedale's three quarries are arranged in line.*

Next objective is the head of Fell Lane climbing out of Cracoe. It is seen just to the right of the village, at the foot of the moor. While you could make a direct descent, a far better way can be found. Head right along the moor from the obelisk, on a clear path for some 160 paces in line with the wall over to the right: at a fork bear left, the path soon becoming a sunken way. This slants gently down the slope, having an early briefly fainter spell where a more obvious way takes over just below. Turn down it past a basic stone shelter, the way unmistakable now as it slants down the fell. *Long since grassed over, these innumerable braided ways are worn deep by the passage of sledges loaded with quarried stone.* This great groove absorbs several other such tracks, leaving the rougher slopes then eventually doubling back to falter in reedy ground before the bottom wall. The intake gate is just along to the left, defended by sheep pens. At this point you depart the access area.

The lane is a splendid green way in its first half, before the addition of a farm track. At a cottage it becomes surfaced, to join the B6265. The Devonshire Arms is just along to the left. *Cracoe marks the barely discernible watershed between Airedale and Wharfedale. Its long, low white-walled pub has a good few years' history behind it and like several others in the vicinity it bears the arms of the family on whose moor you have just been tramping. There is also a very popular cafe just past the pub. More recent additions are an ice cream parlour at a farm shop.*

Cross to the footway and turn right along the busy road, leaving at the first opportunity along a pleasanter back road. *At this junction an old stone guidepost forlornly points to Grassington, Burnsall and Skipton.* This too is left at the first chance in favour of the short drive to Threapland Farm on the left. After crossing the beck turn right through a gate to pass between modern barns and on to leave by a walled track. *On departing the environs of Threapland, eyes cannot fail to be drawn by the devastating scene presented by Swinden Quarry to the left.* Emerging into a field the track runs on through the centre, through a gateway at the end and then swings left to a gate. Don't follow it there, but instead bear right to the corner of the fence in front (note an old limekiln), and follow it along to a ladder-stile at the corner. From the head of this dry, wooded little cleft aim directly across two fields, then bear left above a tiny wood to locate the next stile.

Two narrow fields precede a larger one to Ings House's driveway in front of a barn. From a stile by the barn cross two small fields to stiles, then follow the right-hand wall across a larger field, a track rapidly forming. At the end it passes through a small enclosure then crosses a final field to rejoin the track by which you left Linton. Turn left to finish.

LINTON & THRESHFIELD

START *Linton Falls*   *Grid ref. SE 001631*

DISTANCE *4¹⁄₂ miles (7km)*

ORDNANCE SURVEY MAPS
1:50,000
Landranger 98 - Wensleydale & Upper Wharfedale
1:25,000
Explorer OL2 - Yorkshire Dales South/West

ACCESS *Start from the National Park car park on the cul-de-sac road to Linton church. Linton village is served by bus from Skipton.*

A simple amble through fields between mid-Wharfedale villages

From the car park head along the cul-de-sac lane towards the church, but if saving its charm for the end of the walk (see WALK 8), turn up a short enclosed way before a house on the right. At the top (ignoring another way branching off it) a pasture is entered, and crossed to a stile to the left of the barn ahead. From it rise diagonally up above the steeper drop to arrive at a stile in the distant facing wall. Two slender fields then precede emergence onto the Burnsall road. Turn right a few yards to a gate opposite, and rise left to a gate in a fence at the top corner. *Very evident in the fields hereabouts, and across the river, are a wealth of strip lynchets, cultivation terraces of early farmers.*

Ascend slightly left again to a small gate, behind which a green snicket wends its way up to join the narrow Thorpe Lane. *In an uncharacteristic lapse the Ordnance Survey has omitted to portray this snicket as the enclosed way it has clearly been for a long, long time.* Turn right on Thorpe Lane, but leave it after just a minute at a stile by the remains of a barn on the right. Head away, through a dip to the edge of trees on the brow ahead. Now descend towards Linton, a thin path down the field to a stile in the corner. A track forms to lead to the village, remaining with the right-hand wall until just short of a farm. Here take a bridle-gate on the right and bear left, through another and past the farm buildings to a final gate onto the access road, turning right into the village centre.

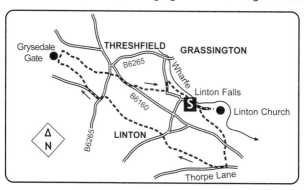

Linton-in-Craven (Sunday name) is accepted as one of the north's most attractive villages, and not without good reason. A rich assortment of limestone buildings stand in laid-back fashion, none wishing to crowd the spacious green. Nearest is the white-washed Fountaine Inn, recalling a local benefactor. Richard Fountaine made his money in London, but in his will remembered Linton by paying for the 'hospital' at the end of the green: this 18th century building continues as almshouses today. Through the green runs Linton Beck, crossed in quick succession by road bridge, ford, clapper bridge and most strikingly, packhorse bridge. Sadly the village's long established youth hostel closed in 2003.

Leave by a track departing from the other side of the road bridge, upstream with the beck past a pinfold. This narrows to an enclosed footway known as Well Lane, before emerging into a field. Here the path forks. Take the left branch to a bridge over an old railway line. *This is the former branch line from Skipton to Grassington, and was in use from 1902 to 1969. It still comes within a couple of miles, but only to serve the quarry at Swinden.* Across, bear right on the path running to a belt of trees, there bearing left with the wall to run through a gateway and remain with the wall to join the B6265. Cross with care, going left a few steps to head off along the side road of Moor Lane. Remain on this just as far as a house, after which take a stile into the field on the right. Head away with the wall, and continue through the centre of this large pasture to find a wall-stile towards the far end. Now slant down towards the house ahead, using a stile just past a gate to emerge onto Grysedale Lane at Grysedale Gate.

Turn right briefly, but before the next house leave by a stile on the right. Drop down to a stile below, and head away between wall and stream. Opening out, cross to a stile ahead, then over a drive-way where it bridges Rowley Beck to a stile opposite. This hides a slab bridge on Spiredale Beck, from where bear right to a corner stile. Now bear right to a stile further round, and continue by a line of trees to the next stile, a path junction. Your way is left, up the wallside with Threshfield appearing. *To your left is the grassy but distinct embanked course of a tramway which carried stone from Threshfield's quarry down to the nearby railhead.* Towards the end is a stile in the wall, from where bear right across this large field to a corner stile in front of houses. Advance down the wallside of this small enclosure to a stile on the left, emptying onto a farm track into Threshfield. *For a note on Threshfield see opposite.*

Re-cross the B6265 to a side road heading away alongside the triangular green, enclosed by walls, shrouded in trees, and hiding the village stocks. Joining the B6160 at the end, turn right on the footway down to a gate on the left from where a path crosses to a bridge on the old railway. A broader track heads away, curving down to Threshfield School. *This fine 17th century building was originally a grammar school.*

Turn left on the road for a few minutes to a stile on the right, where a path doubles back to run downstream above the Wharfe, here flowing wide and calm between two weirs. Grassington Bridge is in view upstream. The path runs into the open to lead down to the tiny Li'l Emily's Bridge on Captain Beck. Across, turn left on a snicket leading to Linton Falls footbridge. *From this fine vantage point the river crashes loudly over a tangle of ledges and boulders. Still known by many as the 'Tin Bridge', the old iron structure (itself not the original metal bridge) was replaced in 1989.* Conclude by doubling back to the road just short of the car park.

THRESHFIELD MOOR

START *Threshfield*   *Grid ref. SD 989636*

DISTANCE *6 miles (9½km)*

ORDNANCE SURVEY MAPS
1:50,000
Landranger 98 - Wensleydale & Upper Wharfedale
1:25,000
Explorer OL2 - Yorkshire Dales South/West

ACCESS *Start from the village green opposite the pub. Parking on the adjacent side roads or on the Burnsall road. Served by Skipton-Grassington bus.*

> *Heather moorland and limestone delights combine in the relatively unfrequented hinterland of Threshfield*

    Threshfield is a disjointed village which is scattered in various directions around the junction of the Skipton-Grassington road with the main updale road. The 'new' part of the village - with its striking Catholic church of modern design - is along the road towards Grassington, but it is the more interesting old corner you see. Solid stone cottages and farm buildings overlook a triangular green, enclosed by walls and shrouded in trees. Inside are some stocks and the flowers of spring. Alongside the green note the stone lintel of the old Post office, dated 1651. Just across the main road is the popular Old Hall Inn, whose title indicates its original purpose. The village school stands down by the river, a former grammar school dating from the 17th century.

    Leave the village by heading south along the main road, over Threshfield Bridge to immediately escape by a stile on the right. Head across this large pasture to find a stile in the wall at the far end, hidden behind a small knoll. Continue away, bearing left to pick up a gentle grassy track, and joining the wall ahead it follows it left until meeting a stile in it. Cross and slant down towards the house ahead, using a stile just past a gate to emerge onto Grysedale Lane at Grysedale Gate. Turn left up the enclosed rough road, rising to a T-junction with Moor Lane just as it loses its full surface. *Look back to see Grassington, Grass Wood, Great Whernside and Buckden Pike all on display.*

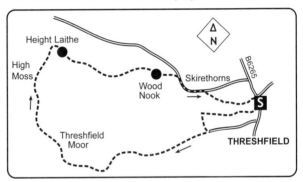

Turn right up the lane to a gate onto the moor. Of the departing tracks take the inviting right-hand one, a bridleway. Passing through a gate in a fence, note the embanked course of a former tramway. *This comes down from the remains of a colliery where poor quality coal was won to fuel the lead smelting operations on Grassington Moor.* Your firm track facilitates rapid progress past the various remains, then rising into the heather of Threshfield Moor. Swinging left where a lesser shooters' track continues straight up, the track rises effortlessly with big views left to Cracoe Fell fronting Barden Moor. As a string of stone shooting butts take shape on the left, the track forks. Here keep left, on a bridle-path where once a moist peaty way is now a firm stride, passing between the butts to run to a wall ahead.

Don't pass through the gate, but turn right to remain on the bridleway on the moor, and at the first opportunity the way enters a walled section through which it runs as a splendid green lane. *This provides glimpses first of Winterburn Reservoir and then of the limestone uplands of Malham Moor.* At the far end it returns to open moor, where another firm path crosses High Moss. *At around 1230ft/375m, High Moss is the highest point of the walk, with gleaming limestone beckoning you on, backed by the broad girth of Great Whernside.*

Slowly descending, an intervening fence is crossed before the path drops to a bridle-gate. Here limestone country is re-entered, as you pass left through another gate onto a short section between walls. Before reaching a barn with a splendidly preserved limekiln behind, turn through the collapsed wall on the right, behind which a stile precedes a wallside descent to the barns at Height Laithe. *Looking ahead to a prominent knoll, note the twin dark entrances of Calf Hole (also known as Height Cave). This has yielded evidence of Bronze Age and Iron Age occupation.*

From a stile at the bottom, cross the yard between the barns and up a short-lived walled green way. At the top turn left through a small gate and head away with the left-hand wall. The grassy path runs to the far corner of the pasture to drop down to Height House, now used as a barn. Beyond it is a stile set into a wall, and on the other side a clear path leads on to the right into Cow Close Wood. *This section is an absolute joy, tracing Rowley Beck down through scattered natural woodland below limestone outcrops. Oak, ash and thorn are interlaced with glacier-deposited boulders, while bluebells add spring colour.* At the bottom a stile admits to Wood Nook caravan site (refreshments), this course maintained down the drive, past the house and out onto Wood Lane.

Turn down the narrow road which swings left at a minor cross-roads into Skirethorns. *Skirethorns boasts a chocolate box scene of cottages across a tiny green.* At a junction with a quarry road, escape by means of a stile on the right. Cross to a stile in the far corner, then bear right around the bottom of two fields to a stile marking a path junction. Your way is left, up the wallside with Threshfield appearing ahead. Towards the end is a stile in the wall. *Just to your left here is the distinctive embanked course of a tramway that once linked the quarry with the now closed railway line at Threshfield.* From here bear right across this large field to a corner stile just in front of the houses. Advance down a small enclosure to another stile on the left, emptying onto a farm track with the pub just ahead.

GRIMWITH RESERVOIR

START *Grimwith   Grid ref. SE 062640*

DISTANCE *7½ miles (12km)*

ORDNANCE SURVEY MAPS
1:50,000
Landranger 98 - Wensleydale & Upper Wharfedale (for full walk)
Landranger 99 - Northallerton & Ripon
1:25,000
Explorer OL2 - Yorkshire Dales South/West

ACCESS *Start from Grimwith Reservoir water company car park, off the B6265 above Dibble's Bridge, two miles east of Hebden.*

A fascinatingly varied trek along a series of old tracks

Grimwith Reservoir was constructed in 1884 to supply water to Bradford, and substantial enlargement in 1983 made it the largest expanse of inland water in Yorkshire. The old footpath encircling it had to be replaced, though in the drought of 1995 we completed this walk on what could have been the original path, such was the absence of water. Improved public access has seen the provision of a car park, WC and quiet water sports facilities. Grimwith is surrounded by rolling moorlands, and in late summer the purple heather makes a fine backdrop.

From the car park turn up the drive between the WC and a small group of houses, and from the gate above a track runs along to the Pateley Bridge road at Fancarl Top. *This windswept moorland track offers a sweeping panorama over Wharfedale to the mass of Barden Moor. As Grimwith Road it was the original access road to the farms of Grimwith House and Gate Up, either abandoned or drowned by the arrival of the deep waters.*

Cross straight over onto a green lane, soon losing an enclosing wall to run an idyllic course to join New Road on a bend. *Simon's Seat rises directly ahead, with the boulders of Fancarl Crag close by to your left.* Go left a very short way along the road to a stile on the right, and beyond a few reeds an inviting green path heads away past a circular pool, dropping gently down to join a grassy former mine track. Before reaching it, note the dark slit that is the entrance to Hell Hole just down to the left. Turn right on the old track just as far as a bend. Here fork left on an inviting green path. *This permissive route links to access land just ahead.* It makes a short pull before crossing the neck of land to drop down to cross a ladder-stile and parallel stream in the upper valley of Trollers Gill. *Trollers Gill itself is along to the right, and can easily be visited: the ravine is explored in WALK 6.*

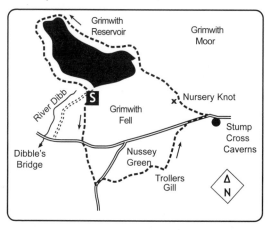

Your route is left, a path slanting up from the beck to a spoil heap and ruined hut at a former lead mining site. *Behind the hut is the stone arched entrance of an old mine level.* Here a superb green track starts to climb away. *To the left note the breached wall of an old dam, while higher up some of the scattered rocks to the left bear the enigmatic cup marks of Bronze Age people, (including a large flat boulder sporting at least a dozen distinctive scoops).* This delectable track rises steadily up the open country of

Nussey Green to a gate in the wall at the top, joining the firmer surface of Black Hill Road. Turn left along here, dropping steadily down towards Dry Gill to join the B6265 Pateley Bridge road.

Turn right along the verge for a few minutes to the foot of the steep pull to Stump Cross Caverns. *Just a couple of minutes further up the hill, these are one of only three showcaves in the Dales, the others being on the flanks of Ingleborough. Discovered in 1860 by miners seeking lead, they ultimately revealed an amazing labyrinth of tunnels and chambers with a display of stalactites and stalagmites that cannot fail to impress. The bleak exterior and setting give no clues to the underground wonders. It is open from mid-March to October and winter weekends, and has a tearoom.*

At the foot of the steep pull to the caverns, a path leaves the road at a small pocket of open ground on the left. After a stile it shakes off its accompanying wall and rises across the grassy moor to the foot of Nursery Knot. The path passes to the right of the out-crop, but few will resist the left branch's closer look. *Nursery Knot is a limestone knoll with sweeping views across the reservoir to Great Whernside, and at 1276ft/389m is the highest point of the walk.* At the wall corner below, two adjacent stiles can be taken in tandem without touching the ground before the path heads off across several rough pastures: occasional stakes point the way to Grimwith Reservoir. Passing through an old wall the path drops down towards the end of a large enclosure, but takes a stile in the left-hand wall before the end to continue its slant. A near pathless, moist pasture is followed by a dry, reedy one before passing beneath an island barn in the first of a couple of green fields to join a rough road alongside the reservoir. *Just back to the left is High Laithe Barn, a cruck-framed, heather-thatched listed building.*

For the short return, head left to the thatched barn, then go right on a more inviting path which runs on the heathery slope before rising to rejoin the hard track, with the start point just a couple of minutes further. The main route embarks upon a circuit of the reservoir, so turn right past the farm buildings of Grimwith House and a side dam where Grimwith Beck comes in. The track winds round past a shooting house up to the right and the ruin of Gate Up on the left. *Evidence of mullioned windows suggests that long ago this was a house of some character. Looking across the reservoir, over the dam is the Barden Moor skyline.*

When the track finally turns to climb to a barn, keep straight on a broad path through bracken to the far corner of the reservoir. *This finest section passes along the foot of two attractive side gills, Gate Up Gill and Blea Gill. During the 1995 drought, the stone bridge beneath where these met was uncovered, a curiously isolated structure sat amidst sun-baked mud.* The path emerges from the 'far corner' and its bracken as a track returns, leading down the west side now. *There are grand views back into Gate Up Gill and the Grimwith and Appletreewick Moors: ahead, beyond the dam, Simon's Seat breaks the skyline.* At a fork the return path is sent down to the left, past a barn and then on as a broader track between walls to the western end of the great dam. A pleasant walk concludes along the top of the relatively unobtrusive grassy embankment to join the road just short of the car park.

High Laithe Barn, Grimwith

Grimwith Reservoir

13

HEBDEN GILL

START Hebden   Grid ref. SE 026631

DISTANCE 3$\frac{1}{2}$ miles (5$\frac{1}{2}$km)

ORDNANCE SURVEY MAPS
1:50,000
Landranger 98 - Wensleydale & Upper Wharfedale
1:25,000
Explorer OL2 - Yorkshire Dales South/West

ACCESS Start at the top end of the village, where the main street joins the B6265. Roadside parking. Bus from Skipton via Grassington.

A fascinating glimpse into the past, ancient and relatively recent. A gentle stroll with just one slightly rough section.

Hebden is a small village divided by the Grassington-Pateley Bridge road. North of the road where your walk starts is Town Hill, a photogenic grouping of attractive cottages and an old bridge. Just up the hill is the village pub, the Clarendon. The bulk of Hebden stands below the road, including the Post office/shop, WC and church which when built saved the parishioners the walk to Linton. The Wharfe is a long way below the village, and is crossed by a suspension footbridge. Hebden, like its bigger neighbour Grassington, grew with the once thriving lead mining industry, with Hebden Gill, and above it Grassington Moor, abounding in evocative reminders of those hard days.

From Town Hill crossroads below the pub, take the unsigned road heading north. The little road becomes a bridleway after the last cottage, though remains surfaced to its demise at Hole Bottom. En route it enjoys the charming surrounds of Hebden Beck before rising over a small brow to drop into the few buildings at aptly named Hole Bottom. Here fork right, on past the last house and right again, through a gate into the open surrounds of Hebden Gill. A good track crosses a charming stone arched bridge, then turns upstream beneath the colourful, craggy flank of Care Scar. Simply remain on this old miners' track all the way along the gill, passing through several gates as the old mining site is reached. On the right is the tall, stone arched Lanshaw Level. Ruins and spoil heaps abound as the surrounds open out at the deep enclave of inflowing Bolton Gill.

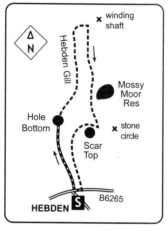

This is the turning point of the walk, so without crossing either beck, take a grassy path beckoning up the slope to the right. *Looking up the deep cleft of this side valley, a dark shadow seen near the top is a former winding shaft from around 1856, restored by the Earby Mines Research Group.* Cross over a stony track and resume a short way up a contrastingly inviting green one. As the dark arch of the winding shaft appears above you might opt to continue up for a closer look: the onward route, however, turns off on a thin but obvious way doubling back to the right. The stone kerbed route of a former watercourse contours round the steep hillside to another arched level just above the stony track. Here the track returns to normal, so advance along it to a gate ahead. *On this contouring section there are increasingly good views over to Barden Moor, with the Cracoe Fell obelisk prominent. Looking back, meanwhile, the upper reaches of Hebden Gill merge into Grassington Moor, with its restored smelt mill chimney in evidence.*

Leaving the mining scene behind, a splendid grassy path heads away through two more gates then rising very gently to be ushered by a wall to a gate at the far end. This admits onto grassy moor, and a super wallside path heads to the far end. The conspicuous outline to the left is the grassy dam of Mossy Moor Reservoir, at a breezy thousand feet up, another relic from mining days, though the water is not seen until reaching the very top. Pass through the gate behind to enter heathery Mossy Moor, and the path runs to a brow. A little further it meets a stony drive to Scar Top House just across to the right. *Opposite this point, some 150 yards off the path amidst dense heather is Mossy Moor's modest stone circle, consisting of four major stones and eight in total.*

At the wall corner, meanwhile, turn to follow the track in towards Scar Top House. Do not enter the private grounds of the house but follow its enclosing wall around to the right to a gateway at the bottom. This is a splendid moment gaining the edge of Care Scar, with a sudden drop back into Hebden Gill. *The dramatic view includes the bulk of Burnsall Fell and the distant outline of Pendle Hill, with Care Scar's tangle of boulders just to the right.* A super little path winds steeply down through the bracken and continues down to a small gate in the wall below.

A thin trod heads off across contrasting green pasture, then slants to the bottom left corner, meeting the wall and running on with it to the far end. Through the stile advance on a field bottom to a corner stile at the end, then a grassy way slants down above the beck to a stile at the far end. Behind it is a footbridge, but remain on this bank on a path downstream to a row of cottages, passing along the front and up over that attractive bridge to finish.

Care Scar, looking over Hebden Gill

GRASS WOOD

START *Grassington*   *Grid ref. SE 002639*

DISTANCE *5$\frac{1}{2}$ miles (9km)*

ORDNANCE SURVEY MAPS
1:50,000
Landranger 98 - Wensleydale & Upper Wharfedale
1:25,000
Explorer OL2 - Yorkshire Dales South/West

ACCESS *Start from the square in the village centre. National Park car park. Served by bus from Skipton, Ilkley and Buckden.*

> *A walk of two distinct halves, on good paths through woodland and by riverbank*

For a note on Grassington, see page 56. From the square head up the main street past the Devonshire Arms as far as a crossroads by the Town Hall. Here turn left along Chapel Street. Part way on turn right up Bank Lane, which quickly loses its surface and swings left as a walled track. At a path junction towards the end, turn left through a small gate, over a plank bridge and across the field to a stile. *While crossing, look right to note an intriguing arrangement of four parallel drystone walls appearing almost on top of each other.* From the stile go left a short way down to another stile.

While the Dales Way goes right on the track here, simply cross straight over to a narrow stile in the wall opposite. Bear right across a large, undulating field to find a similar stile onto the enclosed track of Cove Lane. Ahead is a pleasing arrangement of field walls and barns in front of Grass Wood. Accompany the green lane to its demise, and take the right-hand gate. Cross to the far end of the field, and on to a ladder-stile into Grass Wood.

Although graced with much wooded beauty, Grass Wood is also of major importance in the botanical world, a bewildering variety of flowers being found here. This is the largest individual remnant of native broadleaved woodland in the Dales, and is managed by the Yorkshire Wildlife Trust. Its counterpart Bastow Wood reaches greater altitudes to the right of your path. Just after entering the wood is the site of a settlement of Celtic origin, identified by low, lichen-covered stones.

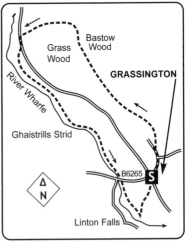

A good path heads up through the trees, keeping right on a broader path at the first fork. The path rises steadily for some time to reach a brow near a wall corner. Now level, the broad, firmer path runs through a clearing, alongside a distinctive trough to a crossroads. The thin path left offers a couple of minutes' diversion up a low limestone scar to Fort Gregory. *This is an Iron Age hillfort dating from AD70, with a well-defined stone base in an open site.*

Back at the crossroads resume along the main path, briefly, towards a broader clearing, but leave the wide track for a less firm one branching right. It maintains a level course through trees with a moss covered limestone pavement on the left, before descending towards the far end of the wood. After a sharp left turn the descent gathers pace, merging into the wide track forsaken earlier. *The drilling of a great spotted woodpecker echoed throughout this section on my last visit.* More easily seen are examples of woodland management such as coppicing, the harvesting of hazel and ash. Continuing down, with the boundary wall close to hand there are splendid views north to Kilnsey Crag. The track ends at Grass Wood Lane. *Here stood the gibbet that hanged Tom Lee, local blacksmith turned notorious murderer two centuries ago.*

Head left a short distance to a stile into the Woodland Trust's Lower Grass Wood. A super path passes through a stile and along the wood edge to the Wharfe's bank. *Looming high on the opposite bank is Netherside Hall, currently a school.* Resuming downstream a super path soon rises onto a higher bank, to merge with another. Further, at an angled cross-paths, bear right on the main one back down to the river and on to a stile out of the wood. Delightful river-bank walking on open pastures leads to a wooded knoll.

Here is Ghaistrill's Strid, like Linton Falls still to come, a rare moment of turbulence for the Wharfe. *A seat invites a longer pause as the river is channelled through a ravine. This takes all the water when the river is low, otherwise the Wharfe rushes through and over rocky shelves alongside.* The path runs to a stile ahead, into a short enclosed spell above the lively river. A couple of stiles further the riverbank is regained to resume across a sidestream and on to approach Grassington Bridge. A track at the top corner runs to a gate in front of a grassy area with seats next to the B6265.

Cross straight over to pass below a row of houses before regaining the same bank of the river. Two weirs are passed before arriving at the less uniform delights of Linton Falls. *Here the Wharfe crashes loudly over a tangle of rock ledges and boulders, and is viewed dramatically from the footbridge just above. Still known by many as the 'Tin Bridge', the old iron structure was replaced by a modern edifice in 1989. New housing has also replaced the former mill on the opposite bank.* After surveying the scene conclude the walk by turning up the narrow snicket (Sedber Lane, also known as the Snake Walk) on your bank, which with good views of Linton church returns you to the main car park.

Walkers approaching Grassington Bridge

15

LEA GREEN

START Grassington   Grid ref. SE 002639

DISTANCE 7 miles (11km)

ORDNANCE SURVEY MAPS
1:50,000
Landranger 98 - Wensleydale & Upper Wharfedale
1:25,000
Explorer OL2 - Yorkshire Dales South/West

ACCESS Start from the square in the village centre. National Park car park. Served by bus from Skipton, Ilkley and Buckden.

Easy walking on lush turf, limestone features in abundance

   Grassington is the undisputed capital of Upper Wharfedale, a thriving community with a good range of shops, pubs and cafes. The fine, cobbled square is the focal point but it is really only the shop window: hidden away is enough interest for a day's leisurely exploration. Grassington boasted an 18th century theatre and a lead mining industry of which its moor still holds much evidence. Buildings of character include the Old Hall and the former Town Hall-cum-Devonshire Institute. Here also is the Upper Wharfedale Folk Museum and the headquarters of the National Park and the fell rescue organisation. Annual events include the Grassington Festival in late June, and Dickensian Saturdays in Advent.
   From the square head up the main street past the Devonshire Arms as far as a crossroads by the Town Hall. Here turn left along Chapel Street. Part way on turn right up Bank Lane, which quickly loses its surface and swings left as a walled track. *Open views look to Grass Wood and the limestone pastures ahead.* At a bend, take a small gate on the left, over a plank bridge and across the field to

a stile. While crossing, look right to note an intriguing arrangement of four parallel drystone walls appearing almost on top of each other. From the stile turn left a short way down to another stile on the right, with a rough track below. Here turn right along the field centre to a narrow gap-stile at the far end. *The next enclosure is the site of a medieval village, with some grassy embankments being discernible.* Curve left to a stile in the far wall, beyond which a further stile admits to Lea Green.

Head directly away, ignoring a very early fork left. Rising gently, continue to ignore other branches as your broad green way enjoys a steady rise to the brow. Now a parallel wall is seen to the right, though your path refuses to fully join it yet. *Advancing on, just to the left you might discern the lines of old walls that are part of an extensive prehistoric field system. Low evening light best reveals traces of these ancient rectangular mounds.* The path finally crosses to a stile in the wall just short of

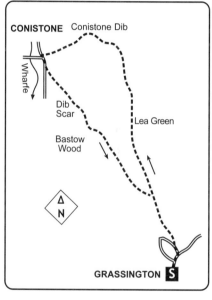

the corner. *Note an old dewpond on the right, created long ago for cattle to slake their thirsts.* Head away to a gate beyond an island outcrop and then rise through bracken to a stile, continuing up past further outcrops to a huge limekiln. *Constructed of immense blocks, like hundreds more scattered about the Dales it was built to provide lime for agriculture. Limestone and coal were put in the top, and burning produced lime for spreading on fields to reduce acidity in the soil.*

The path runs on through the walk's high point to two further stiles, where the path forks. *For the full traverse of Conistone Dib (ascended in WALK 18) bear right to the head of the ravine, where you will find a stile encouraging you into its narrow confines.* The direct route bears left at the fork to descend a dry side arm into Conistone Dib. *Conistone Dib is a classic example of a dry lime-stone valley, narrowing to slender ravines at either end.* Turn left along the green valley floor, and soon the walls of rock close in to form the remarkable gorge of Gurling Trough, a miniature Gordale through which arrival in Conistone seems very sudden. A couple of gates put you on a green at the end of which is the back road to Kettlewell. Just to your left is the village centre. *For a note on Conistone see page 65.*

Leave along the back road to the left, and before the last houses turn up a rough track to the left. *Early in this stage you can enjoy a good view back over Conistone's rooftops to the often dark shadow of Kilnsey Crag.* The track rises pleasantly to the right through several gates before rising more to the left, bound for increasingly colourful limestone country. Directly ahead are the attractive Grass and Bastow woods. After passing through gates in identical wall corners the walk's next spectacular moment reveals itself, as the ravine of Dib Scar appears at your feet. *Dib Scar - or simply the Dib - is another dry limestone gorge, enhanced by a backdrop of woodland, and of sufficient cragginess to have attracted climbers. Above it stands a gem of a sloping pavement.*

The path takes evasive action by swinging left along the rim of the dry valley. At its head a stile takes you over the adjacent wall, across the dip of the dry ravine and up the slope behind to pass through a gap in the next parallel wall. Heading directly away, a stile by a gateway is shortly used to cross the adjacent wall. Back on the pastures of Lea Green, take the path bearing sharply right, with the delights of Bastow Wood just over the wall, though very scattered at this point. *Bastow Wood is rich in botanic interest in addition to its more obvious wooded charm.* A small limestone pavement is passed and Grassington appears ahead. Eventually the wall is forsaken by trending left on a green way, which descends steadily to intersect the outward route just above the stile onto Lea Green. Here drop down to the stile to retrace steps into Grassington.

16

BARE HOUSE

START *Grassington*   *Grid ref. SE 002639*

DISTANCE *5³4 miles (9km)*

ORDNANCE SURVEY MAPS
1:50,000
Landranger 98 - Wensleydale & Upper Wharfedale
1:25,000
Explorer OL2 - Yorkshire Dales South/West

ACCESS *Start from the square in the village centre. National Park car park. Served by bus from Skipton, Ilkley and Buckden.*

> *A walk through splendid limestone pastures
> on the gentle slopes above Grassington*

For a note on Grassington see page 56. From the cobbled square head up the street past the Devonshire Arms to a crossroads next to the Town Hall. Here turn left along Chapel Street. Part way on turn right up Bank Lane, which quickly loses its surface and swings left as a walled track. Remain on this to its demise at a gate/stile, then turn left on an inviting green way rising along the slender field. When it opens out at a wall corner, remain with the right-hand wall to slant to the far end. *Outstanding views look ahead to various limestone scars, Old Cote Moor, Buckden Pike and Grass Wood. You are now on Kimpergill Hill, the site of ancient settlements and field systems that for the most part are barely discernible grassy banks.*

From the stile at the very end, resume with the wall above you, slanting across to a stile in the wall above. The good path maintains this steady slant through a couple of old walls in succession, a stile just behind, and on further across a larger pasture.

59

Only half way on it slants up to a stile in the wall above, and rises diagonally again across another sizeable pasture. *Here you pass a circular walled dewpond created to provide a valuable water source for cattle in these dry uplands: now drained, some concrete grassy terraces remain.* From a stile at the end the path quickly reveals Bare House just ahead, advance to it. *Great Whernside now fully appears beyond, joining its fellow heights of Fountains Fell, Darnbrook Fell, Birks Fell, Yockenthwaite Moor and Buckden Pike.*

The abandoned farm at Bare House is an isolated landmark, having at one time been a drovers' inn: recent years have seen much restoration work. Take the gate to its left and swing right outside the small enclosure behind, to run around to roofless High Barn. From a gate alongside, a track crosses the field to a gate out onto Downs Pasture. Bear right on this track rising to a gate ahead. This admits to a walled green lane, a splendid stride across the walk's high point. Remain on this all the way to meet Old Moor Lane on the edge of Yarnbury. *En route, the smelt mill chimney on Grassington Moor stands tall, with Simon's Seat on the skyline above Mossy Moor Reservoir.* Turn right to the surfaced Moor Lane at Yarnbury. *Just before*

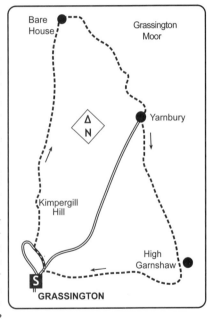

the surfaced lanehead, the way crosses a sloping tunnel driven in 1828 to make a haulage route from a deep mine level. Just over the wall is the start of a fascinating trail around the lead mining remains, more of which are seen on WALK 17.

Lonely Yarnbury was the base of the 19th century lead mining operations, and the sombre Yarnbury House was the mine agent's office: an old weigh house stands in the grounds. Turn right along the road, but quickly take a narrow stile behind a seat on the left after becoming surfaced. Cross to find a stile in the wall beyond, just left of a gate. Rise away to a wall corner, then continue with the wall on the right down a lengthy rough pasture, an improving path passing small quarry workings. From the gate at the bottom continue gently down, a grassy track bearing slightly away from the wall, passing the distinct bowl of a former dam.

From a gate in the very bottom corner rise gently away to the far end, where there is a stile just short of the very corner. Drop onto a clear track just beyond, and turn right along this, soon slanting down to a gate in the corner. Here the walled Edge Lane heads away, initially delightfully green and passing beneath a radio mast to commence a short drop. Soon leave it at a wall-stile alongside a gate on the left. This sends a path slanting diagonally down a string of fields punctuated by wall-stiles, ultimately emerging by a gate onto High Lane. Turn right along this enclosed track to quickly re-enter Grassington at the top end of the village.

The folk museum, Grassington

GRASSINGTON MOOR

START *Grassington*   *Grid ref. SE 002639*

DISTANCE *5³4 miles (9km)*

ORDNANCE SURVEY MAPS
1:50,000
Landranger 98 - Wensleydale & Upper Wharfedale
1:25,000
Explorer OL2 - Yorkshire Dales South/West

ACCESS *Start from the square in the village centre. National Park car park. Served by bus from Skipton, Ilkley and Buckden.*

> *Extensive views add to this fine excursion into the environs of the departed lead mining industry*

For a note on Grassington see page 56. From the square take the road up past the Devonshire Arms to Town Head. Turn right along the front of the Town Hall, and take the first left along Low Lane. At the first chance leave this by a rough lane up to the left, High Lane. As it levels out into a pleasant green way, take a gate on the left and follow a wall up the field to an unobtrusive stile. From here an indistinct path strikes a diagonal course up through a succession of stiles to emerge at a stile by a gate onto Edge Lane. Turning right along it, the walled lane passes a radio mast and improves into a green way to emerge into open moor.

Remain on the main track slanting left up to a brow, with expanding views across Hebden Gill to Care Scar before the walls close in again. The surprise of seeing a farm (New House) ahead is doubled by the appearance of another, High Garnshaw, in the dip just below. Remain on the track (Tinkers' Lane) past the farm, soon rising to a gate on the brow. The way becomes intermittently open and then enclosed by walls: the chimney on the moor is straight ahead. Slanting down the fieldside on a reedy old way, the final stage is enclosed again as the track zigzags down onto the floor of Hebden Gill.

Colourful Hebden Gill was the scene of much mining activity. In the last stage of descent to it, look across into the deep cleft of Bolton Gill to see a dark shadow near to the top. It is a former winding shaft from around 1856, restored by Earby Mines Research Group. Through the gate turn left, immediately through another and along the firm track. This twice fords the tiny beck, pulls through mining debris, drops again, then ascends past a limekiln. Climbing out of the gill to a fork, go right through a gate, and ascending still with extensive spoilheaps over to the left. Ignore any branch tracks to reach a junction with the broad track of Duke's New Road. *At the gateway just before this point, mining features over to the left include the Union Shaft and Beaver Dam.*

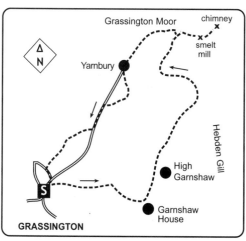

At Duke's New Road the main track bears left for Yarnbury, but the moorland loop awaits: turn right to a gate from where the track contours across heathery Grassington Moor. An embankment at the upper reach of the gill leads to a gate at Cupola Corner. *Here are the remains of Cupola Smelt Mill, built in 1793 and fired by locally won coal. A long system of flues took fumes from the mill to the chimney.* The definitive path ends just before the mill: beyond here be aware of danger from mineshafts and unstable buildings. Through here the track rises away, but at the first bend leave it by bearing right and ascending alongside (but not on) the flue to the chimney. *The chimney stands at the top of the flue system, and at around 1245ft/380m is the summit of the walk. This was preserved in 1971, again by Earby Mines Research Group. Grassington Moor was one of the major centres of lead mining in the Yorkshire Dales, and along with the Pateley Bridge area it rivalled activities in Swaledale. Though dating back to Roman times, the industry reached its peak in the early 19th century, and had virtually ceased before the end of that century.*

Return to Cupola Corner, possibly by way of nearby High Winding Dam, thence down onto the hard track just below. After re-crossing the embankment turn right on a short path to a gate in the wall, accessing the inviting Old Moor Lane. Turn left up its wide walled course, over the brow to reveal Yarnbury just below, where it becomes surfaced. *Just a few steps before the end, the way bridges a sloping tunnel through which ore was hauled from a deep mine level. Grassington Moor Lead Mine Trail offers a detailed exploration of numerous features of interest in the vicinity. At 1150ft/350m above sea level, the bleak setting of Yarnbury would have been much busier when the site of the mine agent's office.*

The traffic-free road, Moor Lane, continues all the way down into Grassington, and though you could remain on it, two successive variations are much more rewarding. The first is a short loop back onto the road: begin by taking a narrow stile on the left after becoming surfaced. Cross to a stile in the opposite wall, left of a gate, then bear right gently up the field to a stile in the wall above. Passing through, you are stood alongside an ancient circular henge, with a grassy outer bank and ditch. Resume to the far corner of the field, where a stile re-admits onto Moor Lane.

Turn left, and just before it starts a steeper descent, take a stile on the right. A trod slants half-right to a gate in the wall ahead, revealing a fine panorama of the Grassington district. A path descends the steep rough pasture to a stile in the right-hand wall. Continue down to a gate in the corner, then resume on the wallside, past Intake Lathe to a corner gate. A green lane (Intake Lane) is joined, enclosed by walls down onto the head of an access road at some houses. Cross straight over, through a stile and down a snicket to emerge onto the foot of Bank Lane. Drop down onto Chapel Street and go left to finish.

CAPPLESTONE GATE

START *Conistone Grid ref. SD 980674*

DISTANCE *7½ miles (12km)*

ORDNANCE SURVEY MAPS
1:50,000
Landranger 98 - Wensleydale & Upper Wharfedale
1:25,000
Explorer OL2 - Yorkshire Dales South/West

ACCESS *Start from the village centre. Limited parking, further room on the wide section of road towards the bridge. The B6160 at Kilnsey is served by Skipton-Grassington-Buckden bus.*

An exploration of limestone country at its best, with a surprise at the top. The going is everywhere easy - not to be missed.

Conistone is an attractive little village avoided by the main road which heads updale just half a mile distant, across the river at Kilnsey. Even from this distance the famous crag loses none of its grandeur. The central junction features a small refuge in which to relax beneath a tall maypole. A telephone box survives, as did a tiny Post office into the 1990s. A pony trekking centre operates from here. Every block of stone in Conistone's many old cottages matches the natural landscape of the village's hinterland. Though restored a century ago, the hidden church of St Mary retains some Norman features, though most poignant is a churchyard memorial to the six victims of the Mossdale Cavern potholing disaster of 1967.

From the main road junction set off along the Kettlewell road, and immediately turn right on a track across a wide green. From gates at the far end a path becomes stony underfoot as it heads up the dry valley of Conistone Dib. After being tightly confined by the imposing buttresses of Gurling Trough the path emerges into the open to pass through a long, green pasture. When the slopes close in again stay with the wall for a short, stony climb to the head of the valley. *Conistone Dib is a classic example of a dry limestone valley, narrowing to very distinctive rock-girt termini.* At the very top the wall is crossed by a stile as it abuts onto a cliff: just above take a stile on the right, and then turn left on a path to a gate which gives access to the wide track of the Bycliffe Road. *A superb limestone pavement sits just above, with a limekiln at its far side.*

Turn right along the Bycliffe Road. *Just before the track becomes enclosed, note a former circular dewpond on the left, created to slake the thirst of cattle on these dry limestone uplands.* As the now enclosed track turns sharp right, leave not by the inviting green way rising ahead, but by a gate on the left. *Bycliffe Road continues to lonely Mossdale, then crosses bleak moors to Middlesmoor village in Nidderdale.* Faint tracks cross the field towards a small plantation, using a

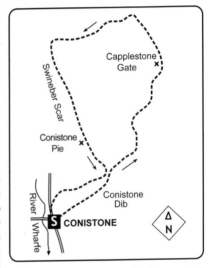

stile to pass its near side. *Your route here is the Conistone Turf Road, bound for the peaty ground above the limestone limit.* The green track climbs to the far end of a prominent scar, and from an old gateway rises more gently to reveal the Ordnance Survey column and scattered rocks at 1680ft/512m on Capplestone Gate.

After the wonders of dazzling limestone it comes as a surprise to meet the sombre gritstone of Capplestone Gate. If your goal had been a hundred feet lower you would not have left limestone, but this dramatic transformation at the 1600ft contour gives a stroll among boulders and old mine workings in complete contrast to the rest of the journey. This extensive viewpoint is arguably the best all-round vantage point for the varied Wharfedale scene. The fell country to the west includes, clockwise: Simon's Seat, Thorpe Fell Top, Cracoe Fell, Pendle Hill, Parson's Pulpit, Fountains Fell, Penyghent, Plover Hill, Birks Fell, Yockenthwaite Moor, Buckden Pike and Great Whernside, of which your viewpoint is a shoulder.

After a well earned rest resume by taking the stile by the gate and turning left along a sketchy path which remains close to the wall running along the bottom edge of the moor. This is your course for some three-quarters of a mile. An area rich in relics of the mining industry is encountered, and the thin path rises a little above the wall through this area. Ignore a stile/gate in the wall at the end of the old workings, and continue along the crest of modest gritstone outcrops as the wall returns. The rocks abate on approaching a stile in an intervening boundary fence, just beyond which it is time to leave the moor. Surmounting a stile alongside a gate in the wall, the world seems to appear at your feet.

A well made old path effects a zigzag down initially steep, bouldery slopes before descending leisurely through a collapsed wall and on through a long pasture. At the very end drop down to leave by a gate near the right-hand corner. A clear track now descends half-right towards a gate into a plantation, but instead of entering, double back left onto a path which bears to the right of an increasing scar to commence a long, level section. A stile in a cross-wall is the first of several encountered, and from it the mini-fortress of Conistone Pie appears directly ahead, the best part of a mile distant. *Across the valley is the often dark shadow of Kilnsey Crag backing the secretive Amerdale Dub, confluence of Skirfare with Wharfe (Amerdale is the old name for Littondale).*

The path runs a splendid course beneath the scars then across more open ground to reach a final stile adjacent to Conistone Pie. *This minor upthrust of rock is a conspicuous Wharfedale landmark, and commands a superb view of the fork of the arrow-like valleys of the Wharfe and Skirfare.* Beyond here another scar materialises to usher you back to the Bycliffe Road above Conistone Dib. Turn right along it - now as Scot Gate Lane - soon descending Wassa Bank past a TV mast which has been in sight at various stages. Becoming surfaced, the access road leads down to join the Kettlewell road, with the village just along to the left, passing the church en route.

MASTILES LANE

START *Conistone   Grid ref. SD 980674*

DISTANCE *8 miles (13km)*

ORDNANCE SURVEY MAPS
1:50,000
Landranger 98 - Wensleydale & Upper Wharfedale
1:25,000
Explorer OL2 - Yorkshire Dales South/West

ACCESS *Start from Conistone Bridge, parking on the wide section of road between bridge and village. Though a start from Kilnsey is possible, parking is very limited: the B6160 at Kilnsey is served by Skipton-Grassington-Buckden bus.*

A famous green road through extensive limestone uplands

For a note on Conistone, see page 65. From Conistone cross the bridge on the Wharfe, and a stile on the right admits to a large pasture. A good track heads away, and when it fades by a wall corner bear away from the river, skirting another corner en route to the prominent barn of Scar Lathe beneath the imposing wall of Kilnsey Crag itself. Here the road is rejoined at a stile, and after appraising the cliff turn left for the brief stroll into Kilnsey.

Kilnsey offers attractions far outweighing its modest hamlet status. It is renowned first and foremost for the stupendous rock architecture of the Crag, whose only fault is its almost unnatural roadside location. It is a favourite climbing ground, and motorists frequently halt to weigh up the progress of rock gymnasts. After rain a clutch of springs gush exuberantly from the base of the cliffs, whose famous overhang broods over Kilnsey's other great draw, its annual show. In late summer the riverside pasture across the road is alive with the colour of the dale's premier event. As with most agricultural shows, the attractions are boosted by such Kilnsey specialities as trotting and fell running. No prizes are offered for guessing the destination of the latter, the senior race being a major event in itself, as back in 1978 when we climbed to see the great Fred Reeves of Coniston touch the highest flag before turning for victory. At the heart of Kilnsey is the Tennant Arms pub. The Old Hall was built in Tudor times on the site of a grange of Fountains Abbey, and has recently been restored to its former glory. Kilnsey Park is a visitor attraction whose features include nature trail, trout fishing, aquarium, shop and restaurant.

Leave the main road by a narrow side road alongside the pub, meeting another road to climb out of the hamlet by the Old Hall. This is an unspectacular start to the 'big name' in green roads of the Dales, Mastiles Lane. *Riding the rolling limestone uplands, it gave access to the valuable sheep grazing grounds of Malham for the Fountains' monks, indeed*

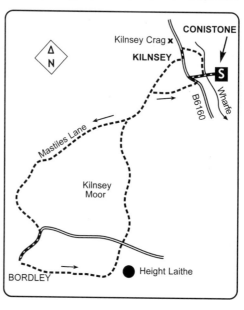

continuing ultimately to their lands in Borrowdale, in Cumberland. Packmen and drovers would have taken advantage of it, though the confining walls that seem integral to its atmosphere would not have been known to its monastic patrons. The road remains surfaced to approach Coolscar Quarry, which rates high in the eyesore league. Fortunately it is escaped by the more inviting rough road branching left before the quarry entrance. The famous lane now remains your chosen course for a considerable time.

Passing below Cool Scar, the old road runs unenclosed a short distance before the walls close in at a depression: on the descent thereto the road can be surveyed ahead, climbing impressively to the skyline. Here the walk reaches its high point at 1388ft/423m. *Ahead, distantly, are the Lancashire uplands of Pendle Hill, Longridge Fell and Parlick and Saddle Fells in Bowland.* From the brow the way drops quickly to Mastiles Gate, and as the road runs free again you leave it by turning left on a grassy wallside track. At the other end is a crossroads with the end of a surfaced road: cross straight over, through a gate, and up the access road to Bordley. *On the brow the hamlet suddenly appears at your feet, nestling in its folds of the hills: down-valley, Winterburn Reservoir is backed by Flasby Fell.* The road becomes surfaced again to drop into the hamlet. *Bordley is a lonely outpost where sheep farming continues much as in its days as a monastic township. Its immediate environs provide an incursion into the gathering grounds of neighbouring Airedale.*

Just before the gate to enter its confines however, turn off left above a wall. *Looking ahead to the nick through which the path runs, note the remarkable contrast formed by the presence of the Craven Fault, with gleaming limestone to the left and gritstone country to the right.* As the wall drops away forge on to drop to a second wall junction in the dip just ahead: a stile awaits. From it a thin wallside path makes the short, steep pull opposite, and as the wall turns off at the brow a grassy track comes in from the left at a pair of stone troughs to forge straight on. The path maintains a straight line beneath limestone scars high to the left, and soon encounters a battery of stiles set in parallel walls. From the last one aim straight ahead towards a barn in the corner. *Note the tiny beck disappearing at Higher Height Holes on the right, and a splendidly preserved limekiln to the left.* A stile deposits you onto an enclosed grassy track above Height Laithe. *Ahead, note also the twin black entrances to Calf Hole (or Height Cave), which has revealed evidence of Bronze Age and Iron Age occupation.*

Head left along the green track, which soon breaks free to cross a lush pasture to Malham Moor Lane, the Threshfield-Bordley road. Directly opposite another track heads off, rising faintly to a minor brow. *Ahead are the dale's twin giants of Buckden Pike and Great Whernside, sadly joined by the view's only blemish, Coolscar Quarry.* The track drops to a gate in an intervening wall. *Just past here on the left is the circular hollow of a dewpond, created to help slake the thirsts of cattle in these dry limestone uplands.* Descent from Kilnsey Moor is by way of a grand track through a shallow dry valley in this vast sheep pasture. Eventually the track winds down to the left, with a brief enclosed spell preceding rejoining Mastiles Lane. *Ahead, enjoy a complete picture of the limestone country above Conistone.*

A direct return to Kilnsey simply involves retracing the first mile of the walk, but to return to Conistone, locate a slender stile at a small kink in the adjacent wall below Cool Scar. From it, wind down to a slab footbridge on a dry stream by the scant remains of a barn. Just beyond, turn left on a track which runs steadily down to pass farm buildings to join the main road. Go left a few yards before escaping along the quieter Conistone road to finish.

High on Mastiles Lane, approaching Mastiles Gate

MOOR END

START Kettlewell   Grid ref. SD 968722

DISTANCE 5 miles (8km)

ORDNANCE SURVEY MAPS
1:50,000
Landranger 98 - Wensleydale & Upper Wharfedale
1:25,000
Explorer OL30 - Yorkshire Dales North/Central

ACCESS Start from the village centre. Car park at the entrance.
Served by Skipton-Grassington-Buckden bus.

*After an early climb this easy walk circles the river and gives
fine views up and down the dale. The return leg calls for
no effort other than that needed to surmount ladder-stiles.*

For a note on Kettlewell see page 81. Leave by crossing the
bridge over the Wharfe at the main entrance to the village, then
forsake the road for the higher of two gates on the right. From it a
good level path heads away, ignoring the Arncliffe branch which
starts an early climb to the prominent notch of The Slit. Your track
remains on the wallside below a low scar and screes: after a level
section it bears left in front of a clump of trees, crosses a tiny beck
and then commences to zigzag up the hillside, ignoring lesser
branches. *At once there is a superb Upper Wharfedale panorama,
to Starbotton backed by Buckden Pike, and back over Kettlewell to
Great Whernside. In no time at all the track resumes its level
course to run pleasantly along to Moor End.*

Up to the left are spoil heaps from the old lead workings. This
second mile of the walk centred on Moor End is a near level trek,
and affords a simply glorious panorama of Upper Wharfedale. The

villages of Buckden, Starbotton and Kettlewell are dwarfed by the immense bulk of three 2000-footers rising beyond the meandering Wharfe. Flanked by Great Whernside to its south and by Yockenthwaite Moor to its north, the central feature of Buckden Pike exhibits various lead mining remains on its slopes. A sheep farm turned outdoor education centre, isolated Moor End is the highest point of the walk at around 1245ft/380m.

Enter the yard and rise above the house on a grassy track to a gate in the top corner. Ignore the track continuing up, and go right a few yards to another gate. Through this cross the sloping field centre on a faint path, through a gate at the end and through a smaller field to a gate through which is a fork. Take the main path slanting down to pass through a bridle-gate in the wall below, joining the Arncliffe-Starbotton bridleway. Through the gate is an exhilarating arrival atop a steep drop to the valley. *This reveals big views over the meandering Wharfe to the finest feature, the combination*

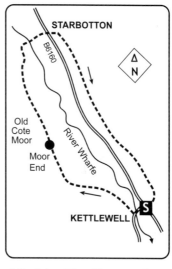

of Starbotton, Cam Gill Beck and Buckden Pike. The way slants gently away from the wall before commencing a steeper, sunken drop into an old wood. It slants all the way down, emerging between hoary, lichen-covered walls. By a barn at the bottom it swings right to a long, wooden footbridge over the Wharfe. Across it a walled path leads along to the road in Starbotton.

Situated midway between the better known villages of Kettlewell and Buckden, tiny Starbotton witnesses all that passes through the dale, even though only a small number pause here. The usual reason for halting is to visit the attractive, whitewashed Fox & Hounds. Off the main road are some lovely corners with 17th century cottages, including a 1665 datestone opposite the pub.

Starbotton nestles beneath the slopes of Buckden Pike, and like its neighbours stands away from the river on its own swift-flowing beck. Cam Gill Beck cuts a deep groove in the flank of the Pike, and in 1686 was swollen by a deluge which caused disastrous flooding in the village.

Walk a yard or two to the right from the point of entry onto the road, and turn up the back road opposite. Use a gate on the right to commence the return to Kettlewell. Follow a track up through three small pastures to enter one with a barn in it, then take a gate just to its left. Now turn right alongside the wall to begin a long, easy march through innumerable pastures, punctuated by a succession of stiles in intervening walls. Throughout its course the path remains virtually level and clear, with a line of unsightly telegraph poles playing their part in pointing the way. When Kettlewell finally appears just ahead the path descends a little towards it, and the village is entered by turning down to the right to a stile onto a short-lived enclosed path. This debouches onto a back road in the village: turn right for the quickest way back onto the main road.

Buckden Pike and Starbotton from the path north of Moor End

21

GREAT WHERNSIDE

START *Kettlewell   Grid ref. SD 968722*

DISTANCE *6 miles (9¹2km)*

ORDNANCE SURVEY MAPS
1:50,000
Landranger 98 - Wensleydale & Upper Wharfedale
1:25,000
Explorer OL30 - Yorkshire Dales North/Central

ACCESS *Start from the village centre. Car park at the entrance. Served by Skipton-Grassington-Buckden bus.*

> *A charming beckside ramble precedes a short and easy fellwalk to Wharfedale's highest top*

For a note on Kettlewell see page 81. From the car park head into the village and leave the main road immediately before the bridge by the two hotels, turning along the road to the right. Fork left at the maypole to pass the church, and at the Kings Head turn right on a lane alongside the beck. At a shapely bridge and former chapel the lane becomes a track, and just further it crosses Dowber Gill Beck. Here leave it by turning up a little beckside path to a stile in the adjacent wall. Now turn right to begin a long mile and a quarter keeping very close company with the beck.

After an early ladder-stile a grand path runs on into the side valley's tight confines as the folds of the hills become deeper. It's just you and the stream, with its occasional little waterslides over rocky shelves. Though the path is occasionally faint, these narrow confines make it impossible to go astray. Great Whernside's upper slopes appear on the skyline ahead, while closer to hand on the opposite slope, a lead mining site includes spoilheaps, ruins and a distinctive old grassy rake. Further, a cliff directly above the path unleashes a sizeable spring, gushing out to supply the greater part of the beck: indeed, above here its course is often bone-dry.

Virtually no height is gained until the unmistakable site of Providence Pot is reached, either by crossing the beck just before it, or remaining on the more enterprising left bank path. *Sited in the centre of the beck, Providence Pot is one of the Dales' better known potholes and is the key to an underground system where the classic Dowbergill Passage links with Dow Cave to the north. An incongruous manhole cover guards the vertical entrance. The slopes above are scarred with the remnants of old lead workings.*

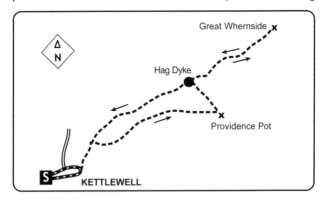

Directly behind is the meeting of twin becks beneath rougher slopes, but your path is the very clear one up the left-hand slope immediately next to the pothole. Re-cross the beck and ascend this super path through the bracken. *This gives superb views down the side valley and back across to old mine workings opposite. Though not a definitive right of way, this time-honoured path is now in any case within open access land.* Higher up, the path takes advantage of a distinctive dry ditch to ascend by. This soon levels out to reveal first the bouldery Hag Dyke Edge up ahead, with Great Whernside's high skyline summit ridge back to the right; then just ahead, Hag Dyke itself. Advance on a thin path to the building. *At 1510ft/460m Hag Dyke is one of the highest buildings in the country, and since 1947 has been put to use as a scouts' outdoor centre.*

Do not enter Hag Dyke's confines, but climb the wide path up the steep scarp to a line of cairns at the top, on Hag Dyke Edge. Great Whernside's summit now appears directly ahead, and the path crosses a moist plateau before a steady climb to the highest point. *Great Whernside is not only the highest of Wharfedale's fells, it is by far the bulkiest. Only from Kettlewell is there easy access. To the east innumerable square miles of bleak moorland fall to the upper reaches of Nidderdale, indeed the Nidd is born within a mile of the summit.* Atop the line of Long Crags - large gritstone 'scrambling' boulders - stands an Ordnance Survey column at 2310ft/704m, and an immense pile of stones, a cairn and a half.

The National Park boundary runs along this summit ridge, which is shared with the Nidderdale Area of Outstanding Natural Beauty. The view is largely one of fells, from the nearby mass of Buckden Pike to the distant Three Peaks, of which Penyghent looks particularly distinguished. A short but lovely section of Wharfedale can be seen from Kilnsey Crag to Grass Woods.

To return to Kettlewell retrace steps to Hag Dyke, and from a gate by sheep pens a small gate to the side of the building sees you emerge at the front. Follow the access track out to a gate, then immediately leave it for an inviting broad, grassy path dropping half-left. At once its course down these splendid rough-grass pastures can be discerned almost all the way, keeping for the most part just above the well-defined drop to your outward route. *There is an early glimpse of Kettlewell in the bottom, with the Hawkswick Moor ridge above backed by the limestone uplands of Parson's Pulpit.*

The path drops down through a collapsed wall and down to a small gate, along a wallside to a stile and on to another small gate. As the wall climbs away and open slopes take over, the path is now firmly atop the steep drop to Dowber Gill. A marker post on the end reveals more of the village below. The descent proper begins here, the path slanting right, away from the gill, down to a gateway, then winds down to a gateway in a crumbling wall, and a distinct grassy fork. Bear right to a stile and continue down this last pasture on a super green way to rejoin the outward route at Dowber Gill Beck. The finish can be varied by crossing the bridge by the old chapel to follow another, parallel back road into the village centre.

22

CAM HEAD

START *Kettlewell*   *Grid ref. SD 968722*

DISTANCE *5³4 miles (9km)*

ORDNANCE SURVEY MAPS
1:50,000
Landranger 98 - Wensleydale & Upper Wharfedale
1:25,000
Explorer OL30 - Yorkshire Dales North/Central

ACCESS *Start from the village centre. Car park at the entrance. Served by Skipton-Grassington-Buckden bus.*

> *A splendid triangular ramble in the heart of the upper dale: uncomplicated and magnificently varied*

For a note on Kettlewell see page 81. Leave the main road through the village by way of the side road heading off opposite the Racehorses Hotel. Cross straight over at the crossroads by the shop (signposted Leyburn) and the road soon swings left to climb out of the village. Within a minute it turns sharply right, and here leave it by continuing up the unsurfaced walled lane straight ahead. This is Top Mere Road, which after a relatively steep start - an excuse to pause to admire the fine retrospective view down Wharfedale - soon eases out to become an outstanding green lane: all that is required is to tread its caressing surfaced way.

In the early stages you pass above the course of a flue from a former lead smelting mill on the floor of the adjacent side valley; while for the most part of the climb enormous colleague Great Whernside dominates across to the right. Eventually all enclosing walls are shrugged off, and the track rises across the fell to arrive at a cairn at Cam Head. *The path running north-east from here*

78

makes for the distinctive outline of Tor Dyke, a defensive earth-work of the Iron Age Brigantes' tribe. The regular appendage of 'road' names to the various green tracks of this walk signifies their importance in times past. Today classic walkers' highways, they originally served more functional tasks, and both the contrasting styles of the Top Mere and Starbotton Cam Roads would be used to reach peat grounds and small-scale lead workings. Their well-laid courses were designed for easy descent with the spoils. The road out of Starbotton was, in addition, on a packhorse route and drove road between Coverdale and Malham.

Here at the 1706ft/520m summit of the walk you encounter the equally inviting Starbotton Road, and after a deserved sojourn, go left along this new green road for a brief level spell. After a second intervening wall the way begins an emphatic descent to Starbotton, now as Starbotton Cam Road. Although this walk's entire upland section is on the accommodating flanks of Buckden Pike, not until now are you granted a true sighting:

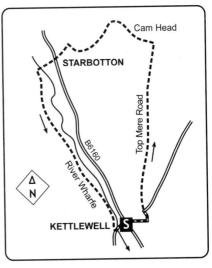

across deeply carved Cam Gill Beck it now makes amends. During this descent the Birks Fell ridge is equally prominent as it forms the dark wall across the valley, which here displays its very finest glacial form. As the dale floor is neared, across to the right note the ruined chimney of Starbotton Smelt Mill, a lead mining relic. Towards the bottom steepening zigzags bear down on the huddled roofs of the village. A stony finish leads onto a back lane, with a number of options for reaching the main road. *For a note on Starbotton see page 73.*

If seeking the Fox & Hounds pub bear to the right, otherwise turn left to the Kettlewell end of the village. Here a walled path heads off right, running to a long, wooden footbridge across the Wharfe. Across, turn downstream and all is plain sailing. *This return saunter on the flat dale floor has many charms: springtime flowers, the winding ox-bows of the Wharfe, a backdrop of high fells, lovely trees, a series of typical Dales barns....* The way, for the most part, is pretty obvious: though the path can occasionally be faint, it is never more than a field's length from the river. When the Wharfe engages in several acute bends, the path tends to short-cut these. *Early on, Moor End is seen apparently delicately perched on the skyline directly ahead.*

Through a string of intervening walls at Haw Fields, the way becomes a good track intermittently enclosed by walls. Crossing a tiny stream at the end of this section beyond a working barn, take a kissing-gate to the left and a part enclosed path resumes. This merges with the riverbank again opposite the village school. When a concrete section ends take a gate on the right and resume on the fieldside, soon returning at a kissing-gate for the final riverside section. The path rises to a track at the end to rejoin the road alongside the bridge at the entrance to the village.

Starbotton smelt mill

LANGCLIFFE EDGE

START *Kettlewell*   *Grid ref. SD 968722*

DISTANCE *5³4 miles (9km)*

ORDNANCE SURVEY MAPS
1:50,000
Landranger 98 - Wensleydale & Upper Wharfedale
1:25,000
Explorer OL30 - Yorkshire Dales North/Central

ACCESS *Start from the village centre. Car park at the entrance. Served by Skipton-Grassington-Buckden bus.*

> *Former mines offer an interesting addition to the meeting of limestone and gritstone in Kettlewell's hinterland*

Kettlewell is the principal village of the upper dale, astride what was a major coaching route to Richmond. The Bluebell and Racehorses at the entrance to the village would have serviced weary travellers, and along with the Kings Head, still do so. Shops, tearooms and plentiful accommodation - including a youth hostel currently doubling as Post office - add more life to a village being engulfed by holiday homes. Kettlewell was a lead mining centre in the early 19th century, and the beck racing through is lined by delectable cottages which would once have housed miners. The village is immensely popular with walkers: footpaths radiate in every direction, by riverbank, through fields, up narrow gills, over the moors, limestone shelves and onto the heights, of which mighty Great Whernside takes a paternal interest. Kettlewell has found additional fame in the 21st century as the principal location for the hit movie 'Calendar Girls'. St Mary's church takes a back seat, with the village stocks and maypole nearby.

From the car park head into the village, and turn on the road to the right before the bridge and hotels. Passing the stocks and war memorial, fork left at the maypole to pass between the Kings Head and the church and straight on along a narrow road parallel with the beck. Just before a shapely bridge carries the road back over the beck, turn steeply up to the right on a stony bridleway.

Through a gate, the roughness underfoot soon gives way to an ever-improving grassy track as the gradient eases. Intervening fence and wall precede a big curve up a large pasture to a higher parallel wall, from where a short-lived way between crumbling walls climbs further. As one wall expires the track zigzags up to the left, then crosses two virtually level pastures to the moor gate and attendant stile. Just down to the left are the remains of the Providence lead mine. *One of the largest in the district, its immediate environs are littered with abandoned shafts and bell-pits. The centre of operations is down towards Dowber Gill Beck, and your track to the moor gate would once have been busy*

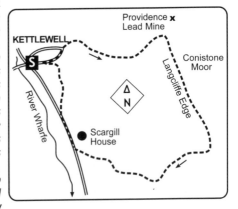

with loads of ore won from the mine. The old workings are - as is the entire walk - on the broad flanks of Great Whernside, which asserts its full stature across Dowber Gill Beck during the climb.

Your route turns uphill with the wall for a short pull to a stand of cairns. *These stone sentinels mark a fine viewpoint for the mountains of the southern Dales, with Penyghent particularly notable. Across Dowber Gill stands Hag Dyke, a scouts' outdoor centre. Almost at the upper limit of the walk you witness the transition from limestone to gritstone, giving a nice change of scene for the stroll along the 1700ft/500m contour. From here on the route, while only a sketchy path, remains infallible as all you* do is accompany the wall along the well defined Langcliffe Edge, with Conistone Moor above. A long mile of walking brings arrival at a ladder-stile/gate, signaling commencement of the return leg. On the other side a wide panorama over Wharfedale greets the eye.

A well made old path effects a zigzag down initially steep, bouldery slopes before descending leisurely through a collapsed wall and on through a long pasture. At the far end drop down to a gate near the right-hand corner. A clear track descends half-right towards a gate into a plantation. Now as Highgate Leys Lane the firmer track descends the hillside, passing near Scargill House before turning left to emerge onto the Kettlewell-Conistone road. *Scargill House is a Christian retreat and conference centre which boasts a familiar Wharfedale landmark in its Scandinavian style chapel, blending surprisingly well into its setting.*

Turn right past the drive to Scargill House, then after a couple of kinks in the narrow lane take a gate by a footpath sign on the right. Follow a wall away to a gate, then turn through it to a gate in a kink in the next wall. Here you commence a fascinating course through some dozen fields within half a mile. *Just up above is a wooded limestone scar, while straight ahead is the walled lane of Top Mere Road ascending the tongue behind unseen Kettlewell.* Though not generally visible on the ground, the way follows a near straight wall, more than once switching to its other side. Kettlewell appears ahead before finally emerging at the head of a snicket on the edge of the village, in front of modern housing. Turn down this pleasant way to a T-junction, with the churchyard straight in front. Either pass through for a look round, or simply turn right along the

enclosed track onto the village back road on which the walk began.

Kettlewell and the Wharfe

HUBBERHOLME & CRAY

START Buckden   Grid ref. SD 942772

DISTANCE 5 miles (8km)

ORDNANCE SURVEY MAPS
1:50,000
Landranger 98 - Wensleydale & Upper Wharfedale
1:25,000
Explorer OL30 - Yorkshire Dales North/Central

ACCESS Start from the village centre. National Park car park. Served by bus from Skipton via Grassington.

A classic valley head promenade, full of variety and interest

For a note on Buckden see page 87. Leave the car park not by its exit, instead use a gate at its northern end from where a stony track gently rises up Buckden Rake. *This is a section of the Roman road that connected forts at Ilkley and Bainbridge. To this day it remains an excellent route, and provides a perfect picture of the dalehead scene, looking beyond Hubberholme's church tower into Langstrothdale, with the Birks Fell ridge behind.* At the end of the surround of trees it turns right through a gate to commence a pleasant, level section. Ignore the path bound for Buckden Pike which soon strikes off to the right.

On drawing level with the buildings of Cray down to the left, take an easily missed bridle-gate in the adjacent wall and drop down a steep field alongside a wall: Cray's pub is directly below. At the bottom a gate leads to Cray Gill, which is crossed by stepping-stones to join the road alongside the pub. *Situated at over 1000 feet above sea level, the farming hamlet of Cray is the last outpost of Wharfedale on the high road over to Bishopdale and ultimately*

Wensleydale. This crossing of the fells is known as the Kidstones Pass, and is the easiest motorable escape out of the valley north of Grassington. Cray's one amenity is the White Lion, a welcoming pub with a flagged floor.

Leave Cray by a farm track immediately behind the pub, and follow it up to the left: keep right at an early fork to pass through a natural limestone floored farmyard above various farm buildings. Having passed through a gate above the last building the way remains level through several fields, aiming for a barn just ahead. Pass to its left then swing right to a tiny footbridge over Crook Gill. The walk from Crook Gill to Scar House is along the short-cropped turf of Scar Top, above a steep drop through ancient woodlands. The scarp is marked by limestone scars and sections of pavement. *The slopes to the north rise more steadily to the height of 2109ft/643m on largely unfrequented Yockenthwaite Moor. Throughout this section you are treated to superlative views down the length of the dale.*

From the footbridge swing left to commence a long, easy mile above the well-defined escarpment cloaked in trees on the left: part-way along, the Wharfedale Cairn beckons just up to the right. *Sentinel of the upper valley and highest point of the walk at around 1180ft/360m, this notable landmark is prominent in many local views.*

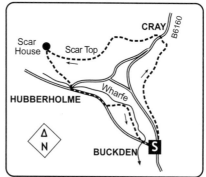

All too soon the path arrives just above Scar House. *Restored in the 19th century, this isolated spot was the scene of early Quaker gatherings.* Turn down between the buildings to accompany the stony access road down the hillside into Hubberholme, emerging alongside the church.

Barely a hamlet, Hubberholme boasts two famous buildings and a shapely bridge which connects them. The church of St Michael is a gem, its tower showing Norman traces. Best feature is a 500-year old oak rood loft, one of only two remaining in

Yorkshire, while some pews bear the famous trademark of the Kilburn workshops of 'Mousy' Thompson. Carving therefore - both ancient and modern - dominates the interior of this highest church in the dale. Outside, meanwhile, the sparkling Wharfe runs almost past its very door. Across the river is the whitewashed and homely George Inn in an idyllic setting. Formerly housing the vicar, its flagged floors continue to be the scene of the New Year 'land-letting', featuring the auction of a 'poor pasture' which originally raised funds for needy parishioners. This was Bradford writer J B Priestley's favourite corner, small wonder that he chose to have his ashes scattered here.

For the final leg of the walk cross the bridge over the Wharfe to the pub, and double back left along the road. After about half a mile take a gate on the left to follow a track along to the river-bank. This soon narrows down into a nicer path, which leads down-stream to Buckden Bridge. Join the road to re-cross the Wharfe back into the village.

The George Inn, Hubberholme

BUCKDEN PIKE

START Buckden   Grid ref. SD 942772

DISTANCE 8^{1}2 miles (13^{1}2km)

ORDNANCE SURVEY MAPS
1:50,000
Landranger 98 - Wensleydale & Upper Wharfedale
1:25,000
Explorer OL30 - Yorkshire Dales North/Central

ACCESS Start from the village centre. National Park car park.
Served by bus from Skipton via Grassington.

*A well-graded and popular climb to Wharfedale's second
highest summit, with the bonus of a beautiful riverside return*

Buckden is the first sizeable settlement encountered by the
Wharfe, and stands at the meeting place of two high roads from
Wensleydale to the north. The B6160 comes via Cray to take over
as the valley road from the narrow, winding strip of tarmac that
reaches nearly 2000 feet on its way over Fleet Moss from Hawes,
before running through Langstrothdale to Buckden. In medieval
times Buckden was the centre of a vast hunting forest, and the
Buck Inn recalls this former importance. The village stands high
above the river on the slope of Buckden Pike, and swift-flowing
Buckden Beck carves a deep defile down from the summit. Apart
from the Buck Inn, there are a couple of tearooms, a shop and WC.

Leave the car park by a gate at its northern end, from where
a stony track makes its way gently up Buckden Rake. *This is one of
the few confirmed sections of Roman road that connected forts at
Ilkley and Bainbridge. An excellent route to this day, it provides a
perfect picture of the dalehead, looking beyond Hubberholme's*

church tower into Langstrothdale. When the surround of trees disappears, the track turns right through a gate and onto the level.

From the next gate however, your chosen path forks right to resume the upward push. As you leave it to climb, note the hamlet of Cray below. The path rises diagonally through five pastures, and beyond the last of them it heads more directly up the open fell. Part marshily it crosses to a wall on the left, some solid path restoration accompanying the wall up to the OS column and cairn on the summit of Buckden Pike. *At 2303ft/702m, Buckden Pike's virtues as a viewpoint are in its distant prospects, which are truly extensive. Most of the major Dales' summits are visible in the western sector, while to the east, moors give way to the flat plains. On a clear day the Cleveland Hills are seen beyond the void.*

To leave the top, use the stile to cross the boundary wall and turn right to follow it along the broad ridge top. Little height is lost as various moist sections are encountered before you reach the landmark of a memorial cross. *This was erected by a Polish airman, lone survivor of a World War Two plane crash on the fell.* At the foot of the slope behind it the track known as the Walden Road is met at a sharp angle in the wall. *This former packhorse route continues over the fell to drop down to the head of the lonely Walden* Valley and ultimately Wensleydale. *Just along it to the left is an inscribed boundary stone.* Use the bridle-gate to re-cross the wall and commence the descent to Starbotton. This is at such a gentle gradient that your time can be employed in enjoying the splendid

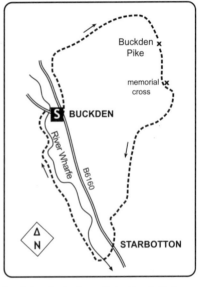

views down Wharfedale. The way is clear throughout: after sloping down across two large, rough pastures linked by some lead mining debris, a cracking pace can now be adopted as the track descends parallel with Cam Gill Beck to your left. Starbotton is entered via a bridge onto a back road. Turn right onto the main road by the Fox & Hounds pub. *For a note on Starbotton see page 73.*

Turn left through the village, and after the last building leave where a gate on the right sends a broad, walled pathway running to the river. A long footbridge carries you over the Wharfe, then turn upstream on a super path through idyllic surrounds. When the river swings off right, continue straight ahead along a wallside, part enclosed old way. At a National Trust sign at a crumbling barn, continue to a footbridge on a stream for a brief enclosed spell. Emerging, the firm path continues, bearing left and across a field centre. Keep straight on, a track forming which soon slants up to meet a firmer track. Advance on this to a barn, and a little further the path is sent down to a gate near a wall-corner from where it drops to the returning river. The Wharfe is now followed tightly all the way to Buckden Bridge, largely on a low embankment. Buckden village is immediately in front. A stile alongside the bridge admits onto the road, cross the bridge to re-enter the village.

Memorial cross, Buckden Pike

26

LANGSTROTHDALE

START Buckden   Grid ref. SD 942772

DISTANCE 6 miles (9½km)

ORDNANCE SURVEY MAPS
1:50,000
Landranger 98 - Wensleydale & Upper Wharfedale
1:25,000
Explorer OL30 - Yorkshire Dales North/Central

ACCESS *Start from the village centre. National Park car park. Served by bus from Skipton via Grassington.*

> Very easy walking in the unspoilt and ravishingly beautiful environs of the infant Wharfe

For a note on Buckden, see page 87. Leave by the Hawes road descending from the green, and immediately over the bridge take the riverside path on the right. This traces the Wharfe upstream until ushered back onto the road. A half-mile stretch leads into Hubberholme. *For a note on Hubberholme see page 85.* Cross the bridge and take a gate adjacent to the church, from where a broad drive climbs to Scar House. *This isolated spot was the scene of early Quaker gatherings.* Passing between the buildings, turn left at the top to a stile by a gate, from where a sketchy path sets an obvious course through the minor outcrops of a limestone shelf. *Throughout this section you enjoy level walking with outstanding views over the youthful Wharfe in Langstrothdale to the Birks Fell-Horse Head ridge which forms a bulky wall opposite.*

Through a small wood the path crosses over Strans Gill. *Under this limestone ravine lurks a complex caving system.* The path then slants half-left before maintaining a level course through numerous walls in various conditions. Further, it is diverted to slant down to a wall before running on through more trees to emerge on a scarred track above Yockenthwaite. The track drops down to the farming hamlet in its magnificent setting. *'Eogan's clearing' was named by the Norsemen who settled here. Much later, all this area was part of the hunting forest of Langstrothdale Chase. Up to more recent times the small community supported both an inn and a school.*

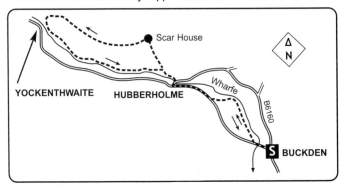

Without descending to the shapely bridge, your return route begins by forking left on a track leading above the lowest buildings. Pass through a gate and a couple more just behind, above sheep pens, then down to a stile just below. From here a path slants down to join the riverbank. *Almost exactly at this point note the lively appearance of a spring, swelling into the river from directly under the bank.* The path now shadows the Wharfe downstream in idyllic surrounds, never more than a few steps from its bank. After a tighter enclosed spell, the way opens out into fields again to see the flat skyline of Buckden Pike filling the frame ahead.

Just beyond a barn the path rises a few feet to negotiate Strans Gill, again by way of a footbridge. At the end of the pasture the path slants a little left to a wall-stile just above, rather than through the gate in front. A little further, the rebuilt path runs along the middle of a steep, scrubby bank, emerging from undergrowth to reveal Hubberholme's church tower right in front. The path runs on to meet the Scar House track just behind the church. Turn back down it into the hamlet, and retrace steps to Buckden.

BIRKS FELL RIDGE

START Buckden   Grid ref. SD 942772

DISTANCE 11 miles (17$\frac{1}{2}$km)

ORDNANCE SURVEY MAPS
1:50,000
Landranger 98 - Wensleydale & Upper Wharfedale
1:25,000
Explorer OL30 - Yorkshire Dales North/Central

ACCESS Start from the village centre. National Park car park. Served by bus from Skipton via Grassington.

> *A strenuous inter-valley double crossing, but a classic. Two valley floor sections through lush pastures contrast with delectable crossings from Wharfedale to Littondale and back. Magnificent views, and a village (and pub!) at all four corners.*

For a note on Buckden see page 87. Leave the village by descending the Hawes road and over the bridge. Continue a little further then go left on a farm drive. Over the cattle-grid, take the right branch zigzagging up the field above Redmire Farm. At the top corner the track passes through sheep pens and onto the foot of the open fell. It runs along to the left through limestone scenery, then at a fork turns right to begin the main climb. *The views back feature the huddle of Buckden nestling beneath the Pike, with the defile of Buckden Beck linking the two.*

The path slants at a steady angle up the hill, encountering peatier ground before effortlessly gaining the edge of the broad ridge top. *Out of sight less than half a mile along to the right is the secretive Birks Tarn, a sizeable sheet of water for its near-2000ft altitude.* A crumbling wall is joined and quickly passed through a gateway, followed a while then a corner cut to join the sturdy ridge wall. Go left with this the couple of minutes to a gate at a junction. This is the walk's summit at around 1985ft/605m, the crossing of the mighty Birks Fell ridge. *At 2001ft Birks Fell was long regarded as the most innocuous Yorkshire mountain, but modern mapping has demoted it below the magical contour. The highest point is an imperceptible rise further to the north-west. The ridge stretches over 11 miles from Knipe Scar in the east to an arbitrary conclusion in Ribblesdale. Over to the left, meanwhile, are the marginally lower cairn and OS column at 1991ft/607m on Firth Fell, just one of many named fells that constitute the full ridge. Looking ahead, eyes are quickly drawn to Penyghent rearing its frame across Upper Littondale: now that is definitely a mountain!*

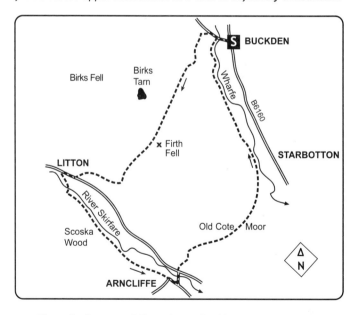

Through the gate follow the wall off the ridge-top, a short level section preceding the long descent. This is steeper than the ascent, with glorious views over the dale, and Litton itself in view.

Leaving the heather moor it continues down with the wall through more lush terrain. Part-way, it loops off to the left to curve back to finally pass through the wall at a gate. It then slants away alongside a hollowed way with Litton directly ahead. The track fades along the bottom edge of a pasture to arrive at a footbridge on Crystal Beck. The green walled way opposite slants down to emerge in Litton just short of the pub. *At the whitewashed Queens Arms, local ales have been brewed since 2003. If it's open, this one will take some passing!*

From the pub head on through the village past the tiny Post office and attractive cottages, and leave the road just beyond the phone box, down a drive to the left immediately before two barns usher the road out of Litton. At the bottom the path runs through a briefly enclosed section to cross a wooden footbridge across the River Skirfare. *The river here is regularly dry, having sunk below ground some distance upstream. Note also the lovely old Elbeck Hall alongside.* Turn downstream to a stile, then cross to a small corner-gate. Turn right alongside a stream, crossing it at a wooden farm bridge onto a drive. Go left a few yards then take a gate on the right. Cross the field to another gate then go left with the wall, continuing to a corner bridle-gate to rejoin the tree-lined river.

A delightful path squeezes downstream alongside a lichen-covered wall, finally emerging at a gate to resume through fields. Through an old wall the river bends away a little: cross a stone slab on a tiny stream and on to a bend of the river. Pass through a small gate in the fence alongside sturdy stepping-stones that are more often than not redundant. Continuing, you pass along the foot of the extensive Scoska Wood. *The largest surviving natural ash, rowan wood in the Dales has been designated a National Nature Reserve in recognition of its importance.* Leaving the reserve, it's back to the field centres, soon crossing a massive pasture which is left by a stile on a projecting corner to the left just short of the end. From the next stile a walled track is joined, and this leads unerringly into Arncliffe, not seen until you are virtually in it.

Cross the road bridge in front to enter the village green. *For a note on Arncliffe see page 96.* Leave by the Litton road, passing the church and crossing the bridge on the Skirfare. Note the return of the river, thanks to springs upstream. At the junction at the end, take a stile in front and climb a couple of steep fields to join a broad track. *Retrospective views over the village, up Cowside Beck and down Littondale are outstanding.* The track winds up through the limestone shelves of Park Scar and Brayshaw Scar, and on to a gateway onto heather moorland. Ignore a left fork to a prominent shooting box, and enjoy the track's climb through a sea of heather.

Suddenly the path levels out and the ridge-wall on Old Cote Moor is just ahead. *It can be seen descending for some way down to the right, while in front Buckden Pike and Great Whernside appear majestically, a stunning prospect.* The walk's second crossing of the ridge sees you reach around 1706ft/520m. Pass through the gate and head directly away on the wallside path. At the wall corner pass through and continue directly down, the path later dropping left to pass through a gateway in a wall. Continue straight down, passing round the left side of a crumbling circular enclosure to find a gate at the wall below.

Turn through the gate to earn an exhilarating arrival atop a steep drop to the valley (see page 74). *Buckden Pike oversees a very complete picture culminating in the strikingly flat dale floor, on which the villages of Buckden, Starbotton and Kettlewell have returned more fully. Best positioned is Starbotton, from where Cam Gill Beck strikes deep into the flank of the Pike.* The way slants gently away from the wall before commencing a steeper, sunken drop into an old wood. It slants all the way down, emerging at the bottom between lichen-covered walls. By a barn at the bottom it swings right to a footbridge over the Wharfe. The track across it offers a detour up to the road in Starbotton *(see page 73).*

Don't cross unless visiting Starbotton, but turn upstream on a super path through idyllic surrounds. When the river swings off to the right, continue straight ahead along a wallside, part enclosed old way. At a National Trust sign at a crumbling barn, continue to a footbridge on a stream for a brief enclosed spell. Emerging, the firm path continues, bearing left and across a field centre. Keep straight on, a track forming which soon slants up to meet a firmer track. Advance along this to a barn, and a little further the path is sent down to a gate near a wall-corner from where it drops down to the returning riverbank. The Wharfe is now followed tightly all the way to Buckden Bridge, largely on a low embankment. Buckden village is immediately in front. A stile alongside the bridge admits onto the road, cross the bridge to re-enter the village.

HEART OF LITTONDALE

START *Arncliffe   Grid ref. SD 931718*

DISTANCE *4¹2 miles (7km)*

ORDNANCE SURVEY MAPS
1:50,000
Landranger 98 - Wensleydale & Upper Wharfedale
1:25,000
Explorer OL30 - Yorkshire Dales North/Central

ACCESS *Start from the village centre, parking tidily alongside (not on) the green, or by the church.*

Delectable valley paths on the flattest of walks

Arncliffe is one of the most attractive villages in the Dales, and the 'capital' of Littondale. Characterful houses stand back in relaxed manner from a spacious green. A 1677 datestone adorns a barn near the traditional red phone box. The unpretentious Falcon maintains this mood, the only pub in the area to serve its ale directly from the barrel. St Oswald's church stands embowered in trees in a beautiful riverside setting. The solid tower dates back 500 years: outside are the village stocks. The house at Bridge End hosted Charles Kingsley while writing 'The Water Babies'.

From the green head west on the Malham road. After crossing the bridge on Cowside Beck, take a walled track straight ahead. This ends at a stile into a field where stone flags negotiate a moist corner. Cross to a stile near the left corner, then cross a vast field which towards the end has a wooden slab crossing a minor trickle. Through a gateway behind, the path bears right to approach the river. Advancing upstream, the Skirfare briefly wanders off again as the path keeps on to a stile. Continue through a gateway in an old wall, and on to a stile through which you enter Scoska Wood nature reserve. *The slopes above support the largest surviving natural ash and rowan wood in the Dales.* The river curves back in to join the grassy path, which leaves the reserve on passing through a gate to which you will return after the 'Litton loop'. For now, cross the river by a series of massive stone blocks. *These are impassable only in spate, indeed, the stones are often superfluous as the river bed is regularly bone dry here.*

Across the river, resume upstream on a good path along the wooded bank until you reach an impasse. Take the stile alongside and leave the river on an inviting snicket. This swings left and starts to kink. Here take a stile on the right and follow the right-hand wall to a stile in it. Continue on the other side to a stile back onto the lane just as it becomes a narrow footway. Litton's pub is visible ahead now. Go straight ahead on the tight footway to quickly abandon it

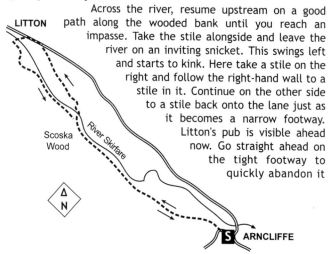

again, at a pair of stiles to enter a field on the left. A gate at the far end accesses yet another walled track, almost at once reverting to footpath width. Further, a track crosses over, though merely to pass from one field to another. Just ahead, again continue along a stony, tightly walled way. At its first bend it becomes overgrown, but a stile makes escape into a field on the left. Slant right, through a stile and across a larger field to a small gate onto the road entering Litton. Go left.

Litton is only the second largest village in the valley of the Skirfare, but can boast that it gave its name to the valley once known as Amerdale. Its attractive buildings are strung along the road, and first encountered is the homely, whitewashed Queens Arms, where local ales have been brewed since 2003 using the pub's own spring. Head through the village past the tiny Post office and leave the road just beyond the phone box, down a drive to the left. Bear left of a short wall at lovely Elbeck House (1707 lintel) to a footbridge on the Skirfare. The river is regularly dry hereabouts, having gone subterranean some distance upstream.

Turn downstream to a stile, then cross to a small corner-gate. Turn right alongside a stream, crossing it at a wooden farm bridge onto a drive. Go left a few yards then take a gate on the right. Cross the field to another gate then go left with the wall, continuing to a corner bridle-gate to rejoin the tree-lined river. A delightful path squeezes downstream alongside a lichen-covered wall, finally emerging at a gate to resume through fields. Though at times faint underfoot, the way is obvious as it heads on through the fields. Through an old wall the river bends away a little: cross a stone slab on a tiny stream and on to a bend of the river. The outward route is rejoined by passing through a small gate in the fence alongside the stepping-stones. Return the way you came, still a lovely walk along the dale floor back to Arncliffe.

Looking up Littondale from above Arncliffe

OLD COTE MOOR

START *Arncliffe   Grid ref. SD 931718*

DISTANCE *6^{1}2 miles (10^{1}2km)*

ORDNANCE SURVEY MAPS
1:50,000
Landranger 98 - Wensleydale & Upper Wharfedale
1:25,000
Explorer OL30 - Yorkshire Dales North/Central

ACCESS *Start from the village centre, parking tidily alongside (but not on) the green, or by the bridge by the church. An alternative is to start from Kettlewell, with its bus service from Skipton via Grassington.*

> *An inter valley crossing on delightful paths: excellent views*

Less than two miles below Hawkswick the Skirfare merges with the Wharfe, and this walk enjoys some unparalleled vistas of substantial lengths of these twin-like dales immediately above their confluence. In both cases, flat valley floors give way to equally well-defined slopes. For a note on Arncliffe see page 96.

From the village green take the Litton (up-dale) road, past the church and across the bridge over the Skirfare. At once leave the road by a stile on the right to accompany the river downstream to another stile onto a back road. From a stile opposite a good path rises diagonally through two fields to enter Byre Bank Wood. *This is an ancient pocket of woodland happily left unfelled due to its steepness. As a result it supports some rarely seen plant life.* The path continues up through the trees to leave by negotiating the modest Pot Scar at the top. *Looking back, a major feature is the deep-cut Cowside Beck just behind Arncliffe.*

Maintaining the same course, the path resumes in easier vein: at a gateway in a collapsing wall a short level section precedes the final pull, and at the second of a pair of neighbouring stiles the ridge-wall on Old Cote Moor is gained. At around 1607ft/490m, this is the highest point of the walk. *Buckden Pike dominates the scene ahead, with uniform looking villages at its foot, while Great Whernside rises protectively above Kettlewell.*

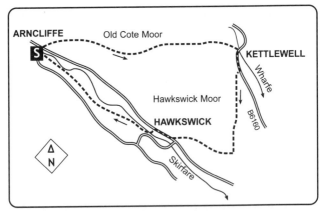

Descent to Kettlewell commences immediately, the initially thinner path inclining right to eventually locate a stile in a wall descending from the moor top. Continuing down at a similar angle a plateau briefly interrupts the drop before squeezing through The Slit, a well-used way through a narrow band of limestone. The path then drops down to merge with another path before reaching a gate onto the road at the entrance to Kettlewell. The route now lies along to the right, though weighing up the prospect of an immediate return climb against the pubs and cafes of Kettlewell, few will resist the opportunity to break journey here. *For a note on Kettlewell see page 81.*

On leaving the village return over the bridge and follow the road a short distance as far as a gate and footpath sign pointing up to the right. A good path heads away, keeping right at a fork and rising through trees to a level enclosure. Bearing up to the right beneath a pinewood, a stile will be found in the top corner, with another just above it. The path then rises through a low scar and continues climbing steadily to a cairn marking the highest point of this return crossing at 1246ft/380m. This lower ridge crossing on Hawkswick Moor permits some intimate views down Wharfedale.

From the cairn the path undulates across to a stile in the ridge wall. Just beyond is another cairn from where the path turns sharply right to begin its descent into Littondale. *Savour glorious views over the valley as well as back down Wharfedale.* A nice, easy decline concludes by entering Hawkswick enclosed by walls. *Hawkswick is the Skirfare's last village, and as the only one off the main up-dale road it remains wonderfully undisturbed.* Turn right past the houses to arrive at a footbridge, and on crossing it take a stile on the right to accompany the Skirfare upstream.

This level return to Arncliffe is fairly straightforward, with an assortment of stiles and gates to point the way. During the central half of this final stage the river largely keeps its distance, though midway it is briefly rejoined at (beware!) a dramatically eroded bank on a sharp bend. The river fully returns by another bend to usher you back to the village, a gate by a barn preceding a short drive emerging by the church.

Kettlewell and Great Whernside from under Hawkswick Moor

PENYGHENT GILL

START Litton   Grid ref. SD 905741

DISTANCE 8 miles (13km)

ORDNANCE SURVEY MAPS
1:50,000
Landranger 98 - Wensleydale & Upper Wharfedale
1:25,000
Explorer OL30 - Yorkshire Dales North/Central

ACCESS Start from the vicinity of the pub. Roadside parking either here or further along the road in the village 'centre'.

> A fine circuit of a lively beck, and a superb green road

Litton is only the second largest village in the dale of the Skirfare, but can boast it gave its name to the valley once known as Amerdale. Its attractive buildings are strung along the road from the whitewashed Queens Arms at the eastern end, where local ales have been brewed since 2003. Litton also has the valley's only Post office. From the pub head through the village and leave the road just beyond the phone box, down a drive to the left before two barns usher the road out of Litton. At the bottom the path runs on through a briefly enclosed section to a footbridge on the Skirfare. *The river here is regularly dry, having sunk below ground some distance upstream. Note lovely Elbeck Hall alongside.*

Across, bear right to a gap-stile just ahead, from where the path crosses two colourful meadows towards a pair of barns at Spittle Croft. From a gap-stile to their right cross the field corner past them to a wall-stile onto an enclosed track. This is followed to the right to arrive at New Bridge. Without crossing it, keep straight on to a gate in front, from where a rough track climbs the hillside. This old road is to be your return route, but for now make use of only a few yards of it then break off across the field to locate a small gate in the wall corner ahead. Across the next field a walled section leads to a barn, past which the path returns you to the water's edge, not the Skirfare but Hesleden Beck just short of its confluence. *Ahead is a first glimpse of Penyghent, soon to be much better seen.* As Nether Hesleden is approached a stone bridge conveys you over the beck, then through a gate turn sharp left to Nether Hesleden. *This ancient settlement is the only habitation between Litton and Halton Gill: note two 18th century datestones.*

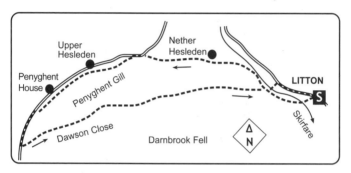

Keep left to pass between the houses to a gate from where two tracks head away. Opt for the more inviting grassy one ascending steeply in front to another gate. Don't pass through, but from the adjacent stile a narrow trod accompanies a fence as it rises above parallel Penyghent Gill. *Majestic Penyghent soon appears ahead, followed by Fountains Fell above your return route to the left. A major feature of the walk is the extended opportunity to survey Penyghent from this lesser known angle, and at 2277ft/694m this crouching lion oversees more than half of the walk.* A level section interrupts the climbing. *Slopes directly across the gill bear the outlines of old walls of an ancient settlement.* A short climb resumes as the fence ascends to the fell road out of Halton Gill.

Turn left along the road for a minute's stroll to a cattle-grid, after which a thin path turns down to a small gate in the wall below. It drops a little further before starting a splendid traverse along the steep flanks beneath Upper Hesleden. Eventually the enclosures below Penyghent House are skirted to arrive at a mini ravine beneath a cave entrance. *Just beneath you, Penyghent Gill is a lovely beck, and unlike much of today's water this section is more likely to be above ground.* Entering a larger pasture at a bridle-gate maintain the same course, rising slightly and on through lime-stone, closing in on the head of the gill. Across a rocky tributary, a grassy mound in this final enclosure is the ancient burial site of the Giant's Grave. Don't pass through the gate ahead, but bear left to a stile near the corner, and advance along the wallside to join the open road. Turn left for a few minutes to the start of the bridle-road which doubles back sharply left across Dawson Close to Litton. *At around 1360ft/415m this high point and turning point of the walk is a good one to linger over, perhaps on the minor rocks just above, savouring in particular the stirring prospect of Penyghent.*

Striding out on the old road, no further instruction is needed as it will lead you unfailingly back to New Bridge. *This outstanding example of a green road has, like many packhorse routes, escaped being surfaced, to remain one of the most distinguishable features of the Yorkshire Dales.* Sometimes open, sometimes with a wall for company, it contours the flank of Darnbrook Fell for a considerable time before finally starting its brief descent, initially through an enclosed section. *Litton appears ahead during this spell, which offers glorious views from above Halton Gill to below Litton.* The outward route is joined just short of New Bridge, and the opening half-mile or the quiet road lead equally clearly back to the village.

Penyghent from Penyghent Gill

31

HORSE HEAD PASS

START Halton Gill   Grid ref. SD 880764

DISTANCE 8 miles (13km)

ORDNANCE SURVEY MAPS
1:50,000
Landranger 98 - Wensleydale & Upper Wharfedale
1:25,000
Explorer OL30 - Yorkshire Dales North/Central

ACCESS Start in the centre of the hamlet. Parking area opposite the green (honesty box). Don't park on the green.

A stiff inter-valley walk in the heart of the Dales. The filling is a couple of peerless miles in the company of the infant Wharfe in Langstrothdale. Save it for a clear day!

For a note on Halton Gill, see page 108. Leave the green by the Foxup road, and beyond a bend after the last buildings take a gate on the right. *At the outset the bird's-eye views of Halton Gill are first-rate. During the climb, the Three Peaks of Ingleborough, Penyghent and Whernside appear in turn: Fountains Fell is also a shapely offering.* A broad track slopes up the field, and this same track remains your route, with little effort and no complications, to the summit of Horse Head Pass on the broad ridge top, with a gate waiting in the boundary wall. *To the left is the OS column at 1985ft/605m on Horse Head, one of several 600m tops along the crest of this mighty ridge. The pass itself climbs little short of the highest point, which narrowly fails to make the 2000ft mark on Birks Fell further east. The well-made green road over the pass was a regular route of Halton Gill's curate, who rode over on horseback to take the service at Hubberholme.*

Descent to the promised land of Langstrothdale is equally straightforward, the track heading directly away from the wall over Horse Head Moor and soon dropping more directly towards Hagg Beck. *These delightful environs herald the welcome appearance of limestone: its attendant bracken and gnarled trees add colour and character to the backdrop of Yockenthwaite Moor and Buckden Pike. The deeply carved gill also holds interest for cavers.* After this stretch Yockenthwaite appears below, and a sometimes thin, grassy path concludes the descent at the unfenced road near Raisgill. Turn left the short distance to Yockenthwaite. *The slender bridge leads to this farming hamlet in a magnificent setting.*

Cross the bridge, and on rising to the first building turn left to a gate. So begins a magnificent ramble in the effervescent company of the Wharfe, often dry at Yockenthwaite after sinking below ground just upstream. At once a well preserved limekiln is passed. After a couple of

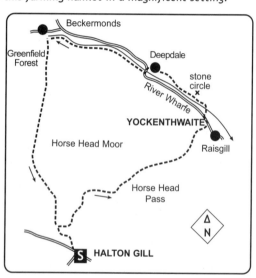

pastures the track fades as it passes Yockenthwaite stone circle. *This compact group of 30 stones is of modest proportion in a noble riverside setting.* From a stile at the field-end beyond it, with a barn ahead, the thin path rises away from the river through a wall gap to another stile. Cross the field-top to drop to a footbridge at the other side, then on through an old wall and a little gate to join the access road serving Deepdale, a small farming hamlet.

Turn down to the road and cross the uninspiring bridge to keep the motor road at bay. A track shadows the west bank to lonely New House, where a path takes over. This proves to be a classic, unbroken riverbank spell as the Wharfe tumbles happily over limestone ledges. Further on the road climbs away, so only your path keeps faith with the river as far as a wooden footbridge opposite the farm buildings of Beckermonds. Beckermonds presides over the meeting of Oughtershaw and Greenfield Becks - the creation of the Wharfe, no less. This confluence is reached just short of the footbridge. *The walk's turning point is a charming spot for a break on the grassy bank, a haunt of wagtails. Beckermonds is backed by Greenfield Forest, home to a herd of Roe deer.*

Don't cross the bridge, as your route must make its way back over the ridge. The climb begins from a gate on the left just short of reaching the bridge and the plantation. A rough track climbs to a barn just above, after which a thinner but clear path ascends the near side of a small beck. *Breaks in this return climb provide wide vistas over the bleak head of Wharfedale.* The stream fades on gentler slopes just short of a series of limestone boulders and shakeholes. The path resumes from the right-hand end of these, and is reasonably easy to follow up the higher slopes, including a spell marked by cairns where it undertakes a brief slant up a distinct groove to the left. Above this the going eases and a stone platform is reached, sadly the well-constructed stone man once atop it has toppled. The ridge-wall at around 1876ft/572m is now visible just beyond, and a ladder-stile quickly gained.

On the other side a delectable green, briefly level path heads directly away. *Arrayed ahead are Darnbrook Fell, Fountains Fell, Plover Hill, Ingleborough, Greenfield Knott and Whernside.* The path swings down to the left to drop steeply through an old wall. Below this it turns sharp left as a level trod, running to a ladder-stile in a descending wall. Remaining level a little further, and crossing over a faint climbing path, the way negotiates a small moist area to slant gently down before improving into a fine green way. This drops down through a modest rock gateway to a hollow above a colourful area of limestone boulders. From a stile in the descending wall ahead, a thinner continuation slants down to a stile in the bottom corner of the enclosure, and a grassy way drops back onto the outward track to finish as you began.

UPPER LITTONDALE

START Halton Gill   Grid ref. SD 880764

DISTANCE 5¹2 miles (9km)

ORDNANCE SURVEY MAPS
1:50,000
Landranger 98 - Wensleydale & Upper Wharfedale
1:25,000
Explorer OL30 - Yorkshire Dales North/Central

ACCESS Start in the centre of the hamlet. Parking area opposite the green (honesty box). Don't park on the green.

Easy walking, good beck scenery, bleak Pennine surroundings

Halton Gill is the first settlement of any size in Littondale. Its cluster of greystone buildings include a centuries-old chapel and even a grammar school, both now private dwellings. Also on show are Church Cottage with its 1626 datestone, next to Church House, the former church of St John the Baptist. A classic red phone box survives. From the junction by the green turn down the Stainforth road and over Halton Gill Bridge, then leave by a stile on the right to descend steps to the riverbank. Accompany the Skirfare upstream through the occasional gate or stile. After a pair of plank bridges, take a stile in the adjacent fence to resume upstream to a wall-stile. This is delightful rambling as the riverbank opens out, with a particularly lovely moment where the river tumbles over limestone ledges. A little further, the path squeezes between sheep pens and river to emerge onto the road at Foxup Bridge. Here the moorland streams of Foxup Beck and Cosh Beck combine to create the Skirfare, though both are not always in evidence thanks to the vagaries of limestone country.

Turn right over the said structure and immediately left on a broad track. Quickly emerging into the open, early on you pass a charming scene where a tiny arched bridge spans the lively beck as it tumbles over limestone ledges. This rough farm road heads unerringly up the valley beneath a grassy fellside, gradually rising above Cosh Beck's grand company to pass between two small alien stands of trees. At the second you can espy Cosh itself, just past a third stand which is not on the map. Eventually (and unexpectedly, in the end) the track arrives at Cosh, the first building since Foxup.

At around 1378ft/420m, Cosh is Remote: geographically it stands at the very heart of the National Park, but it couldn't be further from the centre of things! A thriving farmstead in the early 20th century, it spent many unoccupied years, though it has now undergone restoration. Interestingly, Littondale's highest building is only a five-mile walk from Horton-in-Ribblesdale's railway station, a trek undertaken by former occupants. The name Cosh is of Norse origin, and was once a grange of Fountains Abbey.

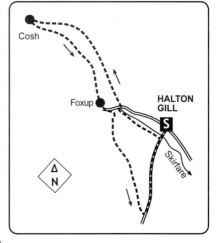

Without entering the confines of Cosh, turn off the track to commence the return journey on a thin path descending towards the beck, but only as far as the brink of the steeper drop to the water's edge. Maintaining this level, head downstream as far as a crumbling, sizeable square stone sheepfold which was probably seen on the outward journey. At this point descend to the beck, fording it and continuing downstream to an immediately intervening wall. From the stile in it rise very slightly across the large rough pasture to locate a stile in the next wall.

From here you enter the fields, already with a glimpse of Foxup ahead: cross to a clever corner stile in the farthest corner ahead (not as per map), then on above the wall to pass above a restored barn. Keep on through a gateway just above to reach another barn, and on through its yard to find a stile in the corner beyond. Now you simply contour on through a series of wall-stiles, virtually parallel with the beck below. Eventually Foxup appears ahead, and a wallside leads to the last stile to cross to the nearest buildings.

A stile and gate to their left give access to a track which drops down to Foxup Beck, crossing it to the road terminus and Foxup Bridge Farm. *Foxup is a farming hamlet marking the upper limit of the valley's surfaced road, comprising five residences at the last count. From here the walk's final couple of miles provide grand views both down the dale and also across to Halton Gill nestling beneath Horse Head Moor.*

Don't continue down to the bridge, but leave the road by a gate opposite Foxup Bridge Farm, with its shapely arched bridge and 1842 dated barn. A track winds up the small enclosure to a gate above. *Looking back over the farm's fair setting, note the intriguing scene immediately updale, where green fields, drystone walls and barns on the southern flanks of Cosh Beck contrast strongly with sombre brown moorland on the north side.* The now fainter track ascends a large pasture towards a gate in the rising wall.

At this bridleway junction don't pass through, but continue up the grassy track. It soon levels out to contour left to a gate in the far corner above limestone outcrops. Through this gate head away just above the left-hand wall, which drops away but leaves the splendid grassy path to march on. *Continually grand views look both down the dale and across to Halton Gill. Ahead is the dark wall of Darnbrook Fell, beyond the unseen rift of Penyghent Gill.* Remaining level, a large pasture is crossed to another gate, the path then running on above the low outcrops of Hesleden Bergh to merge with the Stainforth road. Turn left, utilising the grassy verges for a straightforward descent into Halton Gill, a clear target in the valley bottom.

WALK LOG

WALK	DATE	NOTES
1		
2		
3		
4		
5		
6		
7		
8		
9		
10		
11		
12		
13		
14		
15		
16		
17		
18		
19		
20		
21		
22		
23		
24		
25		
26		
27		
28		
29		
30		
31		
32		

INDEX
walk number refers